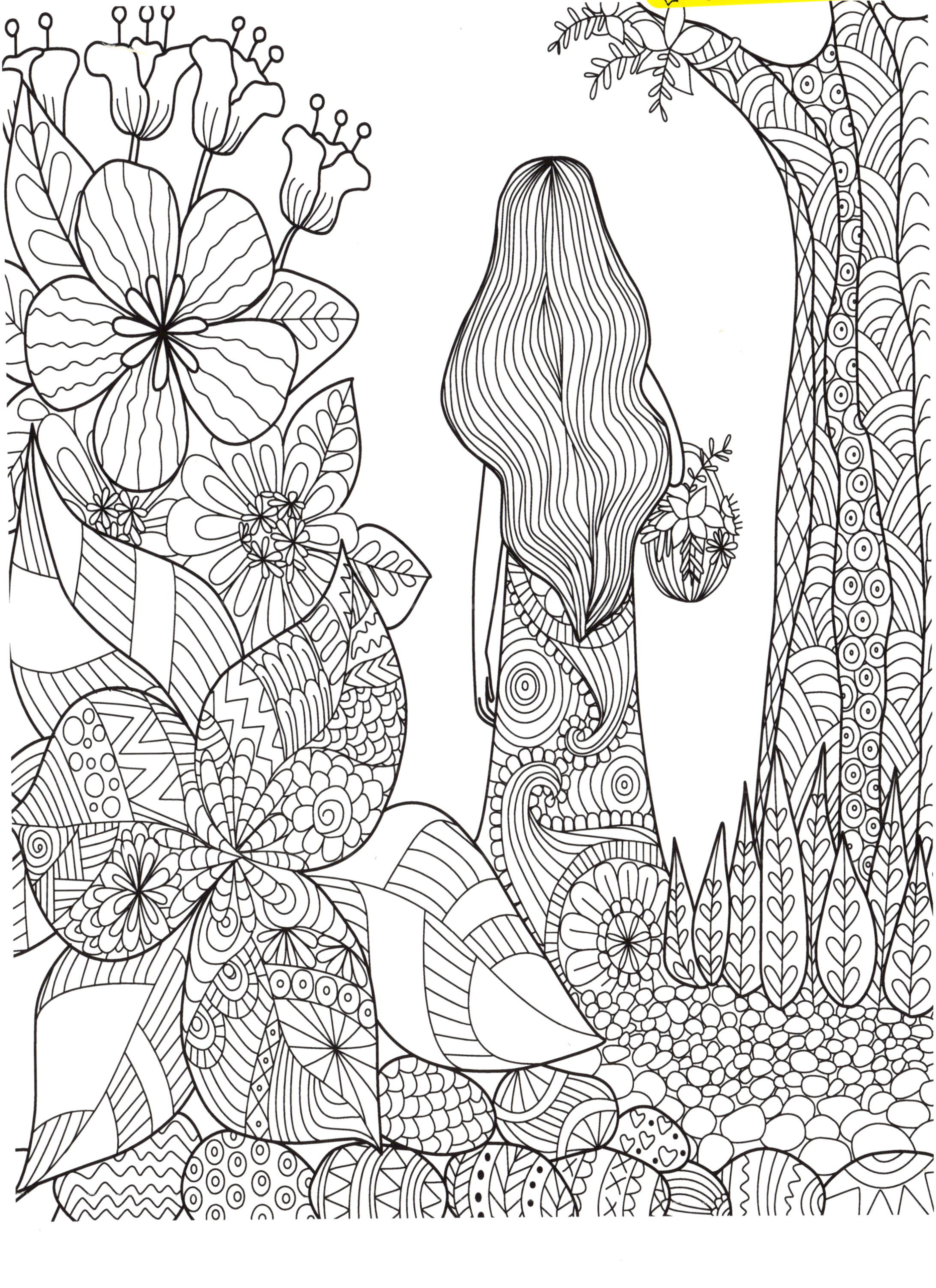

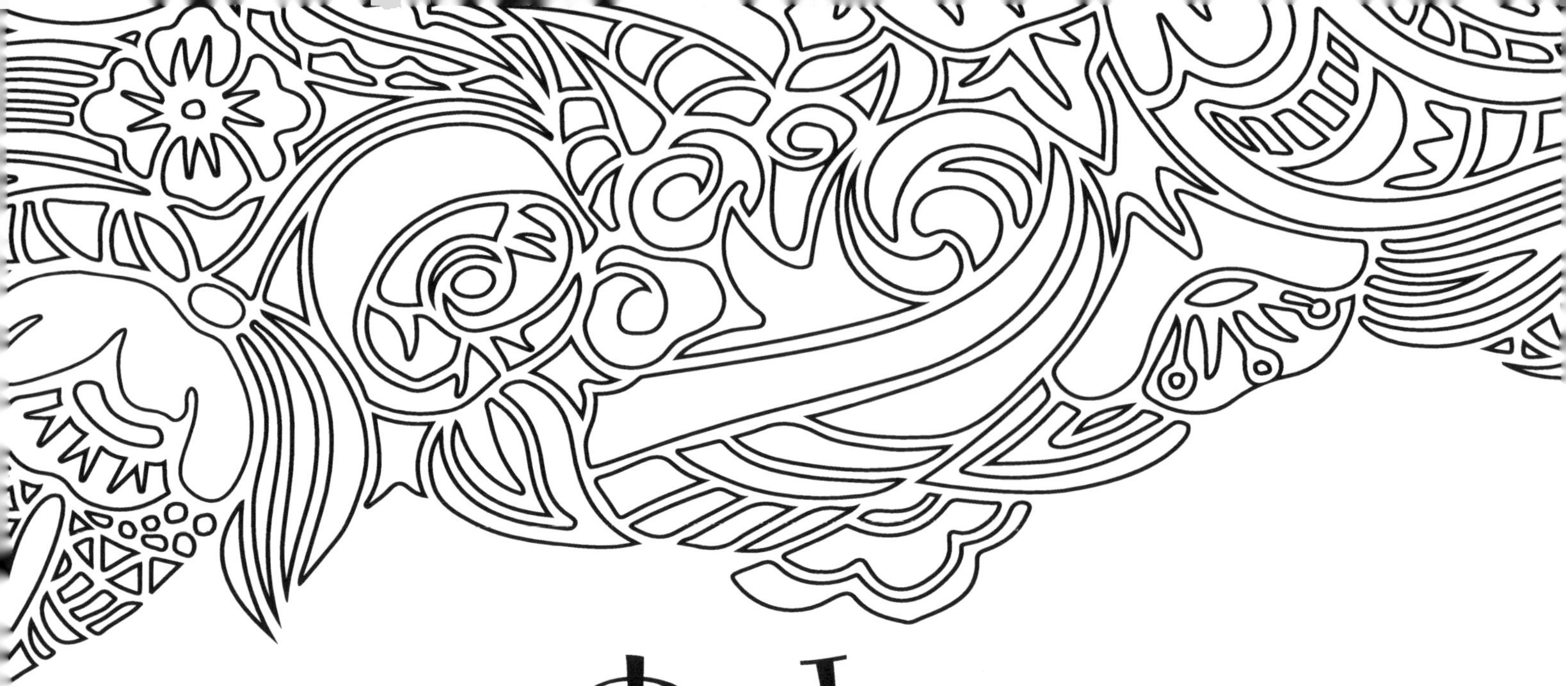

Boho Flower Child

Adult Coloring Book

Sandy Mahony & Mary Lou Brown

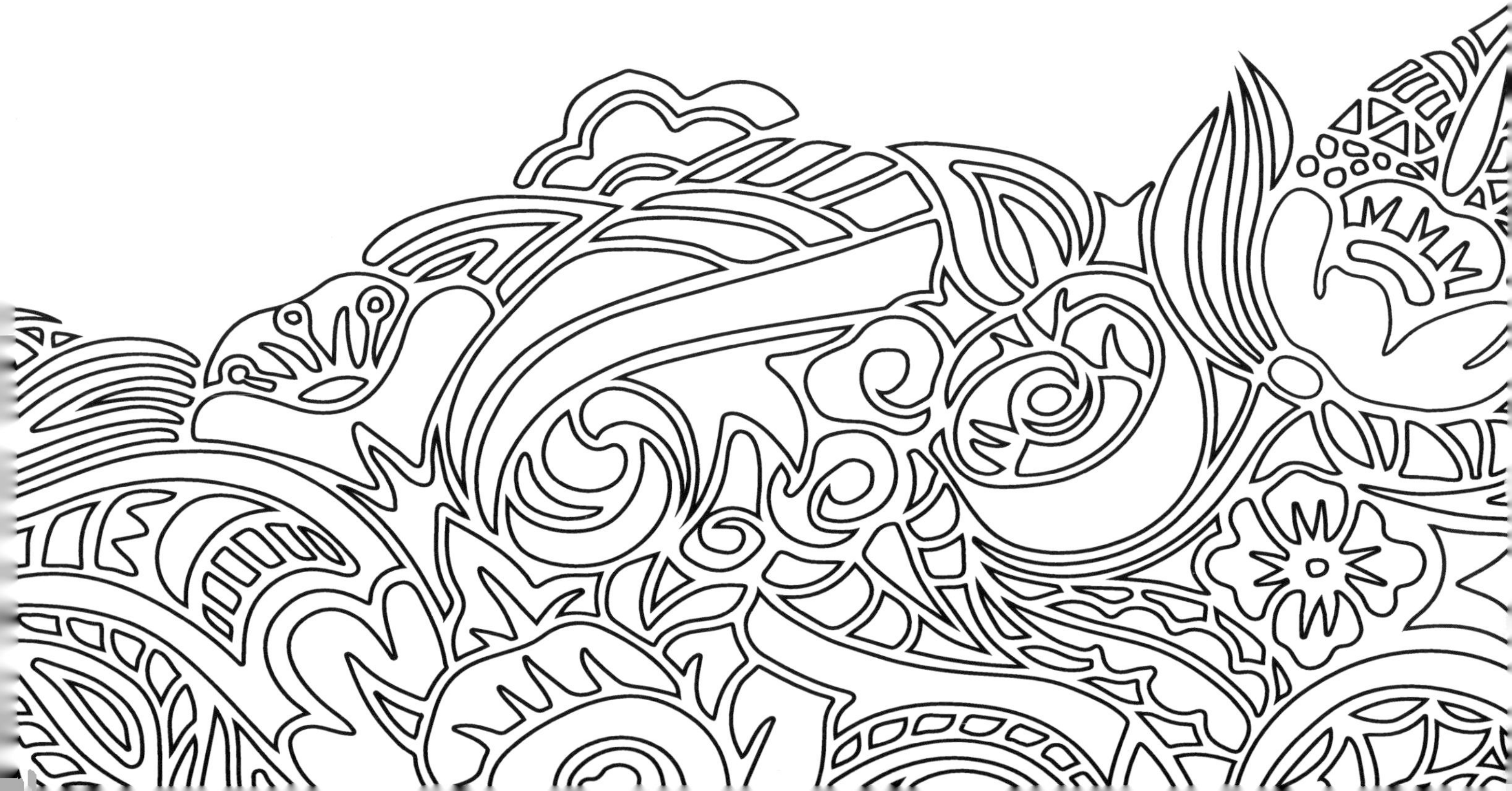

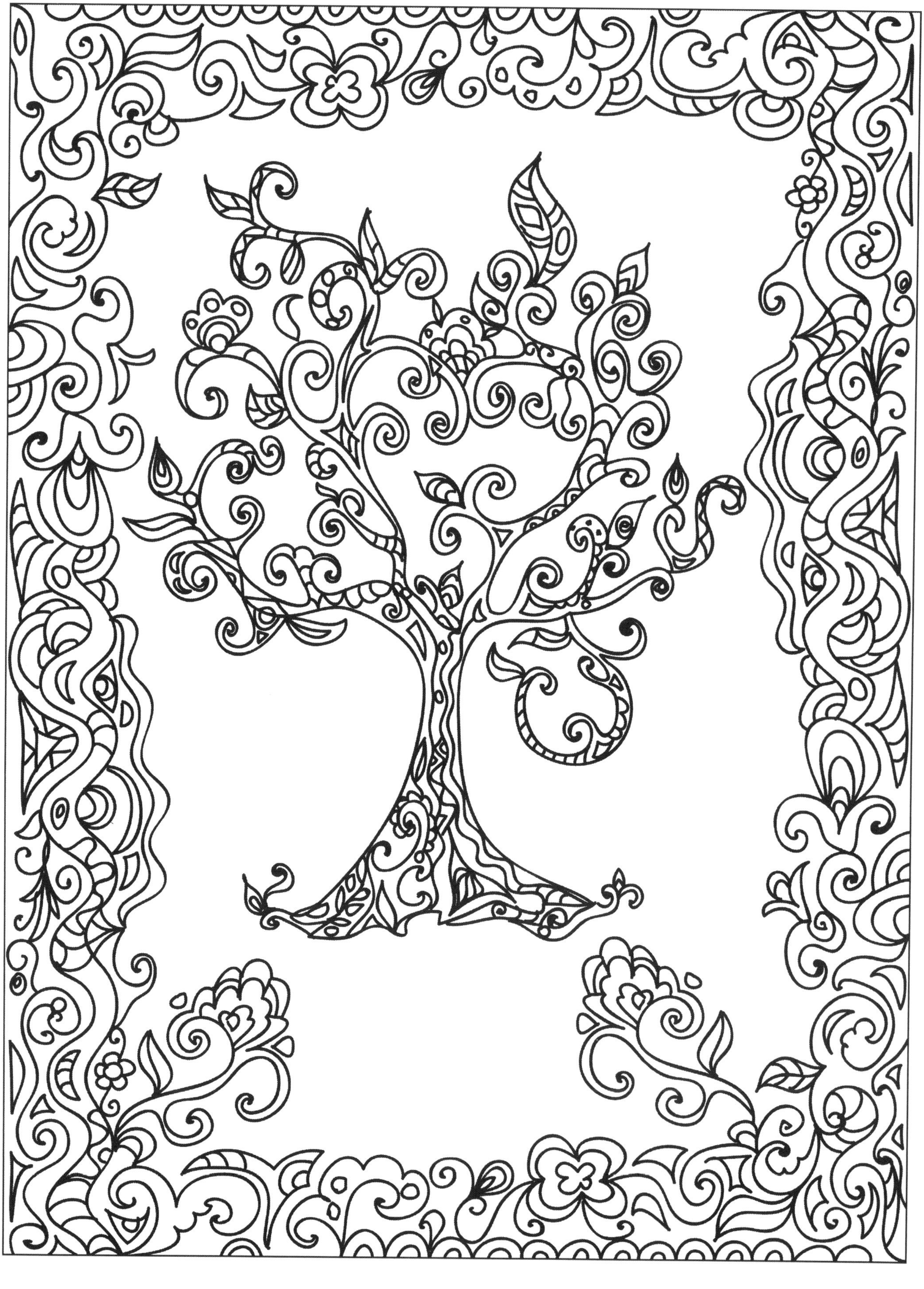

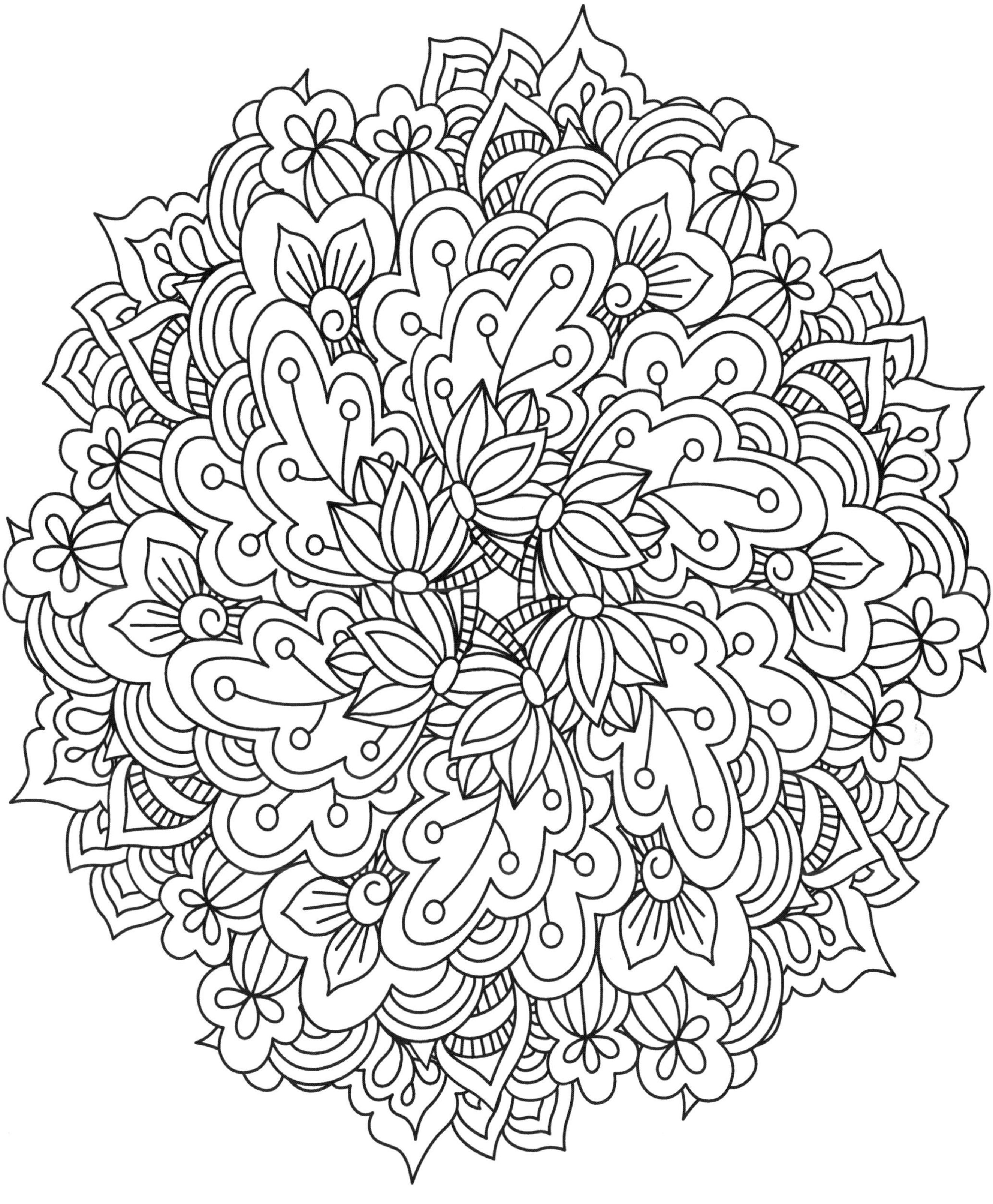

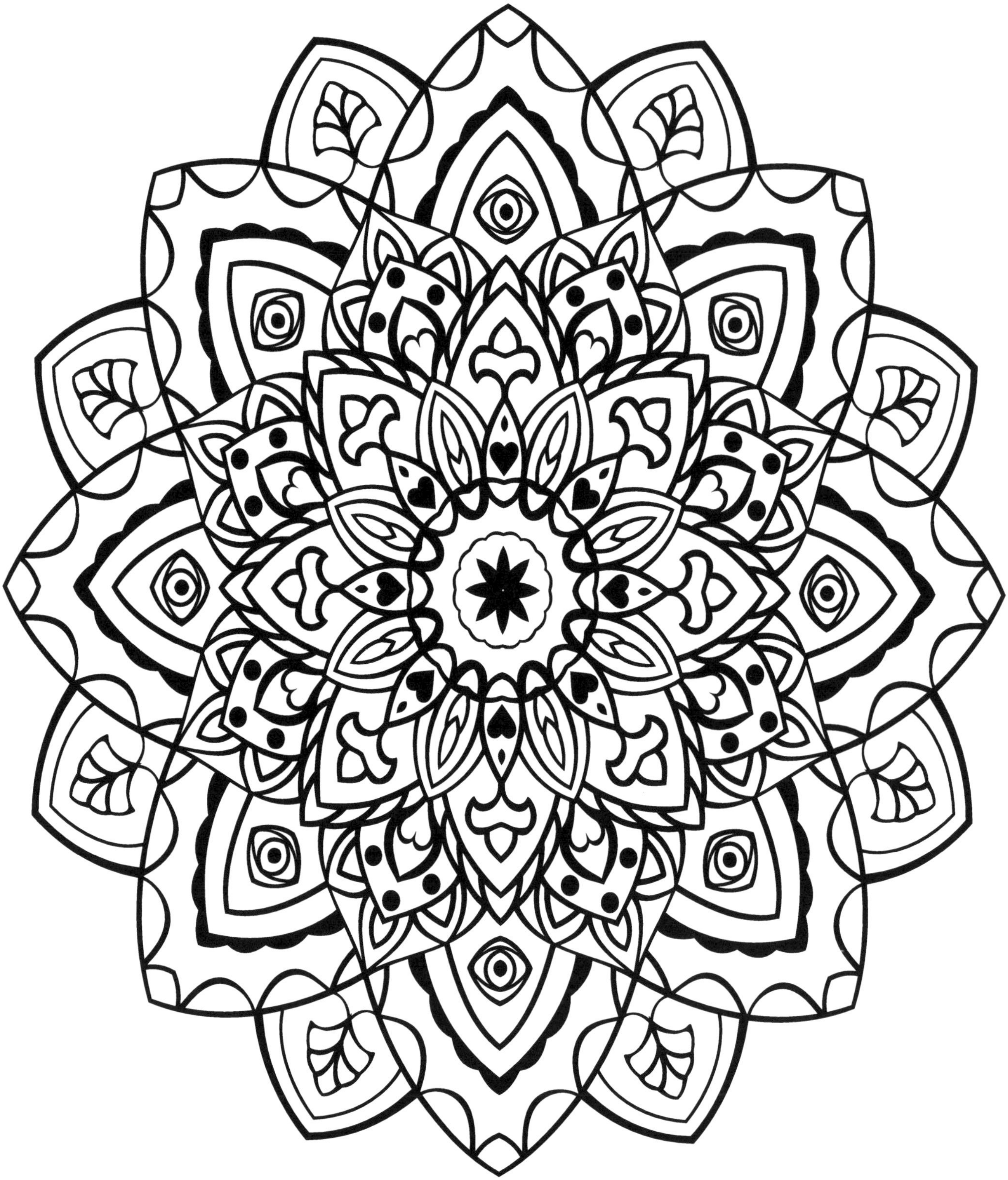

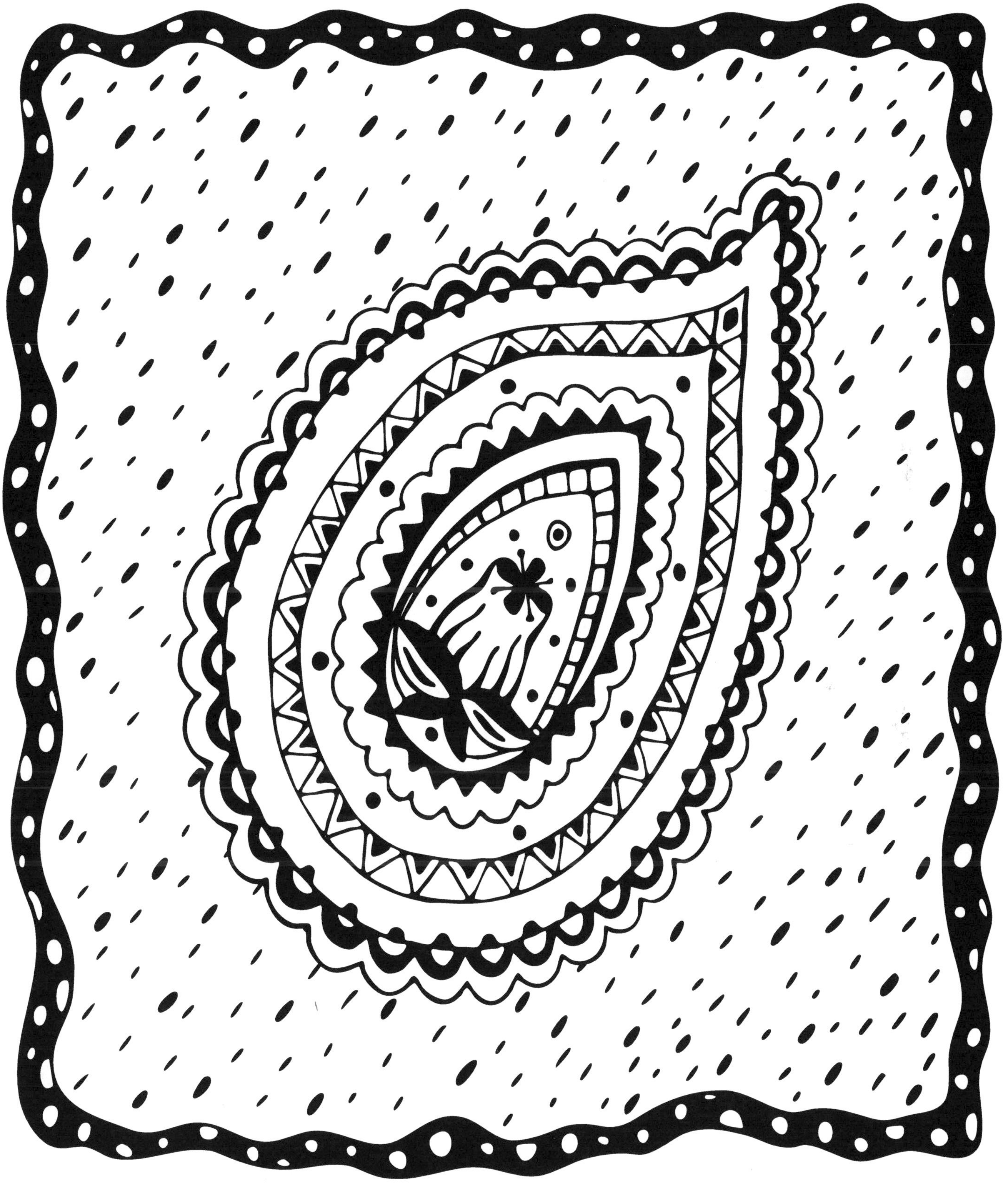

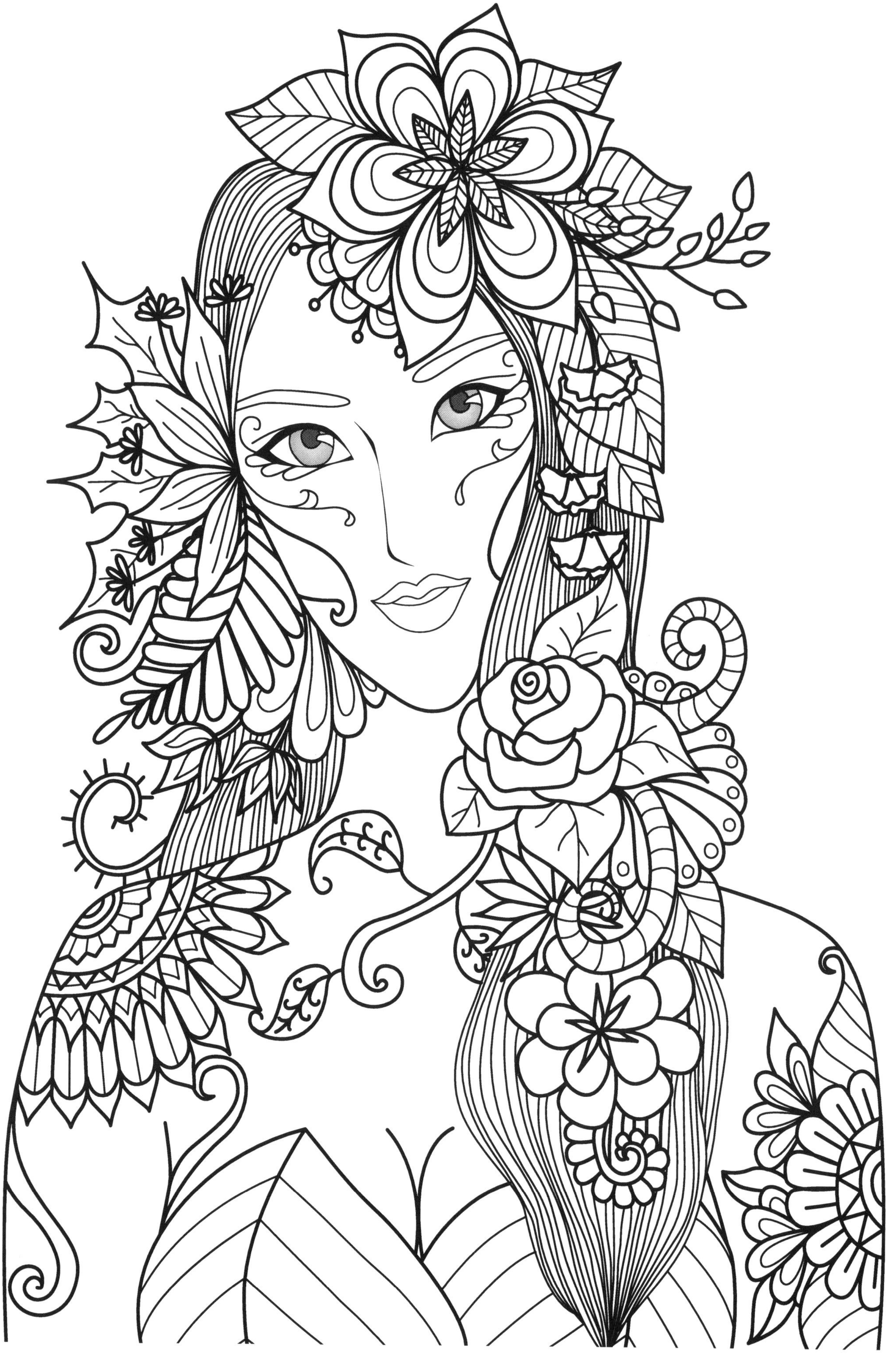

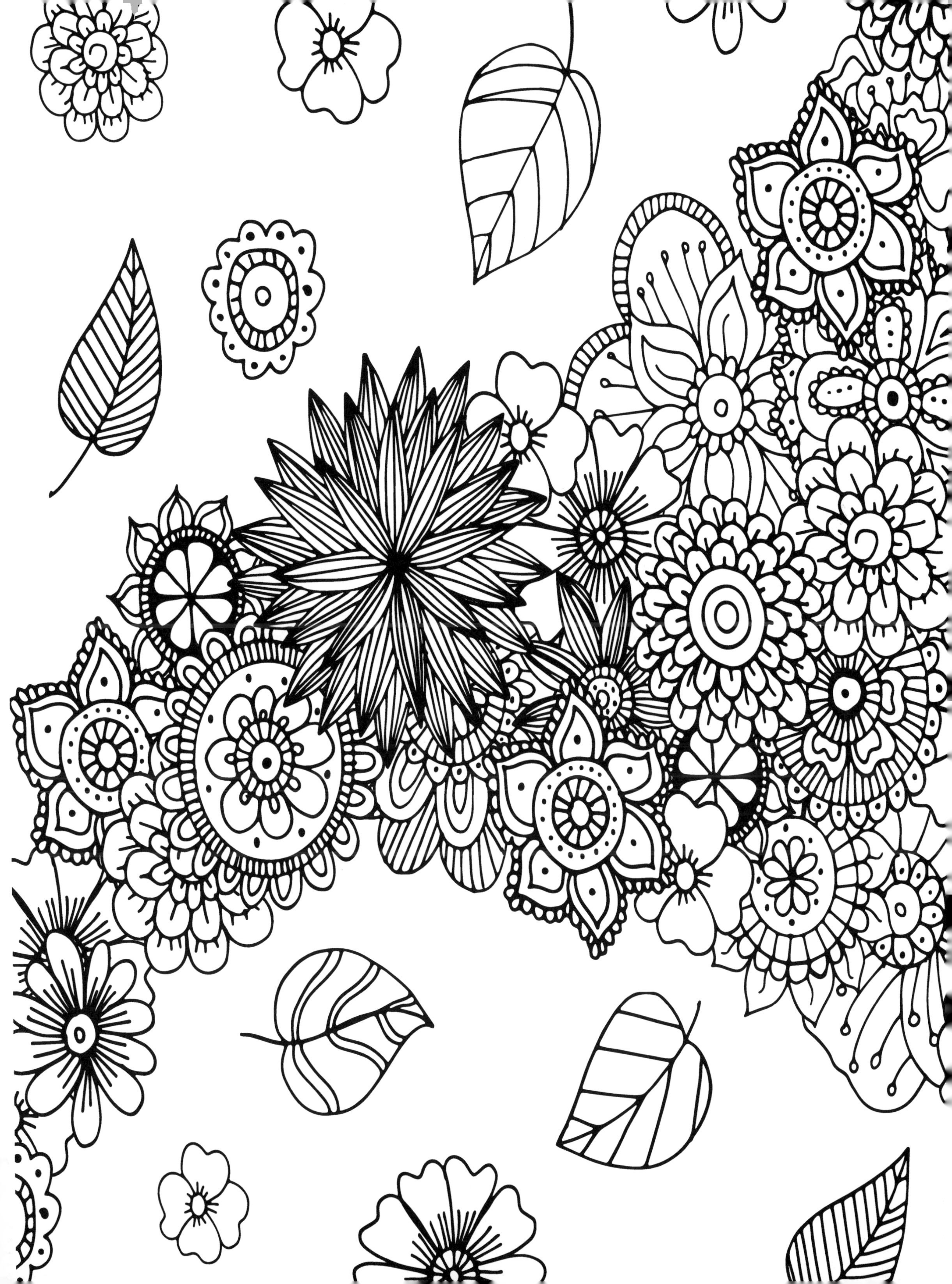

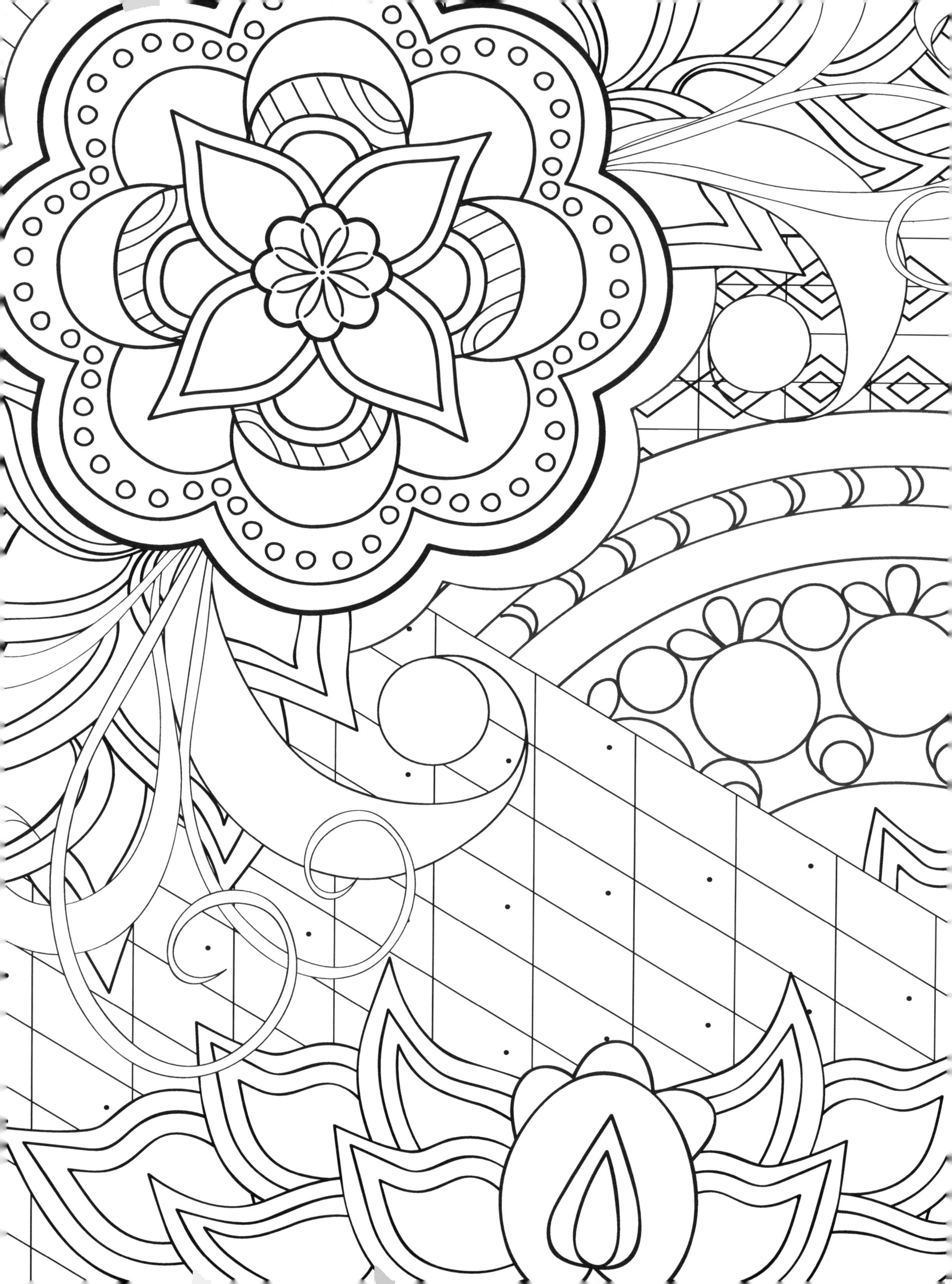

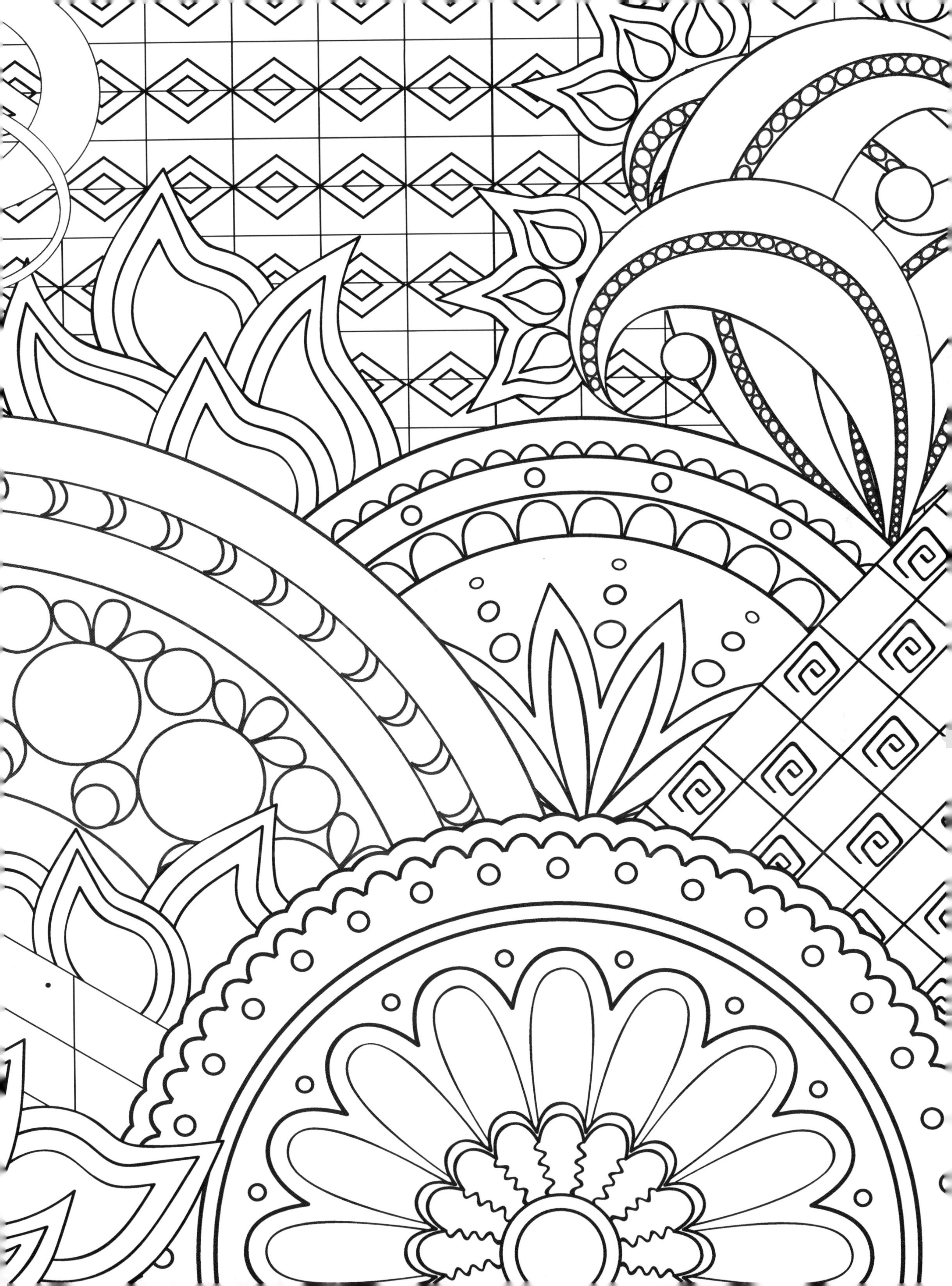

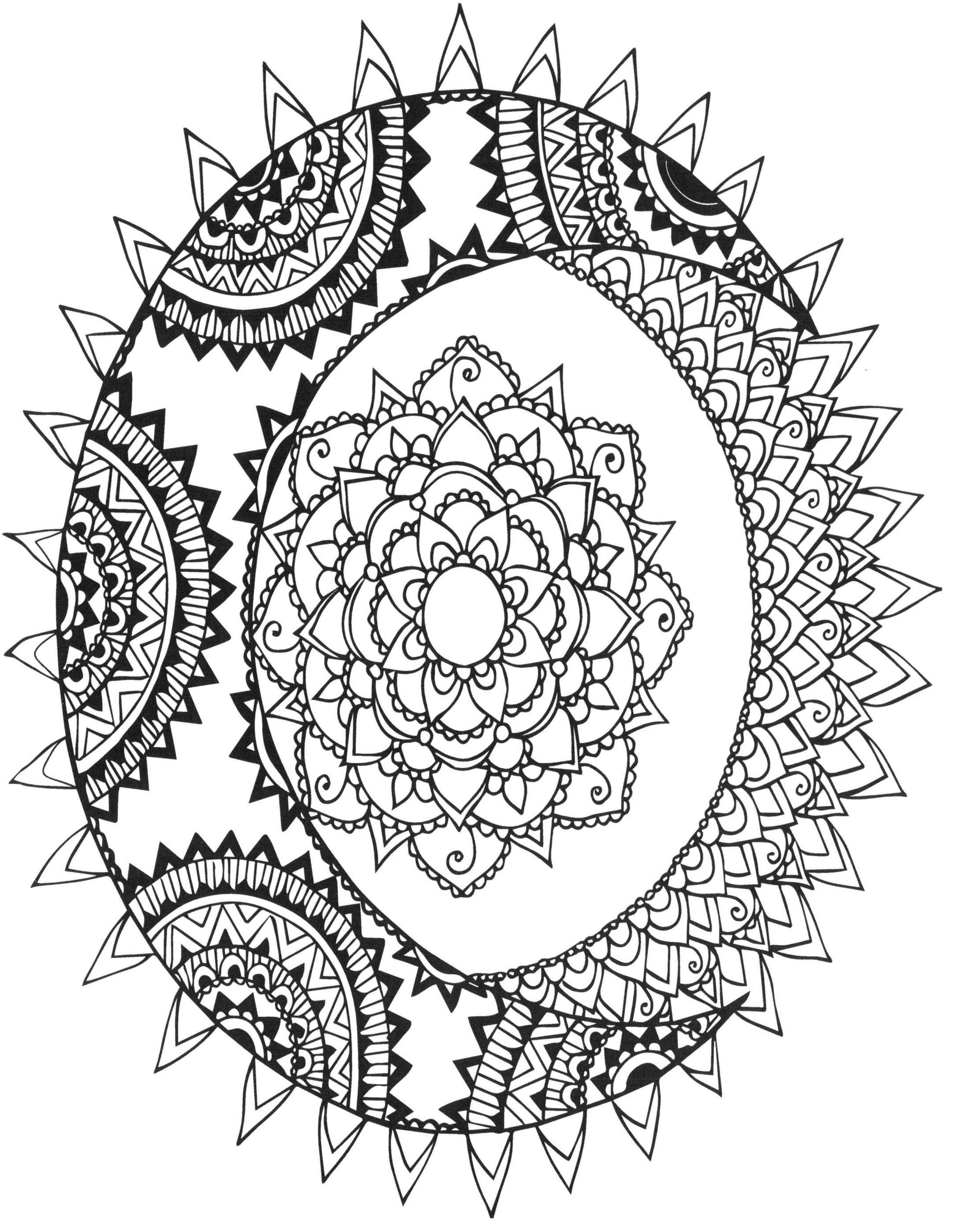

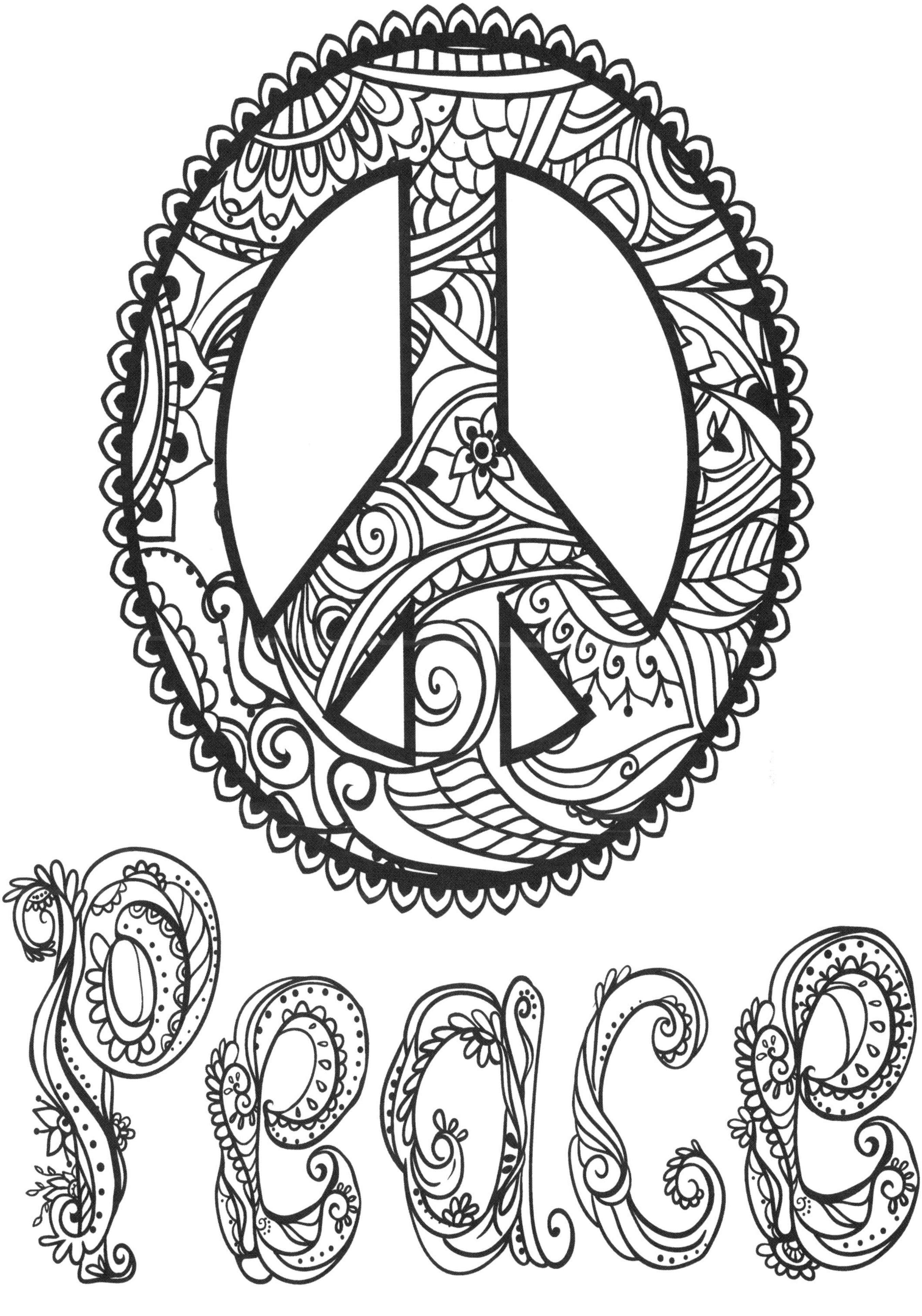
Peace

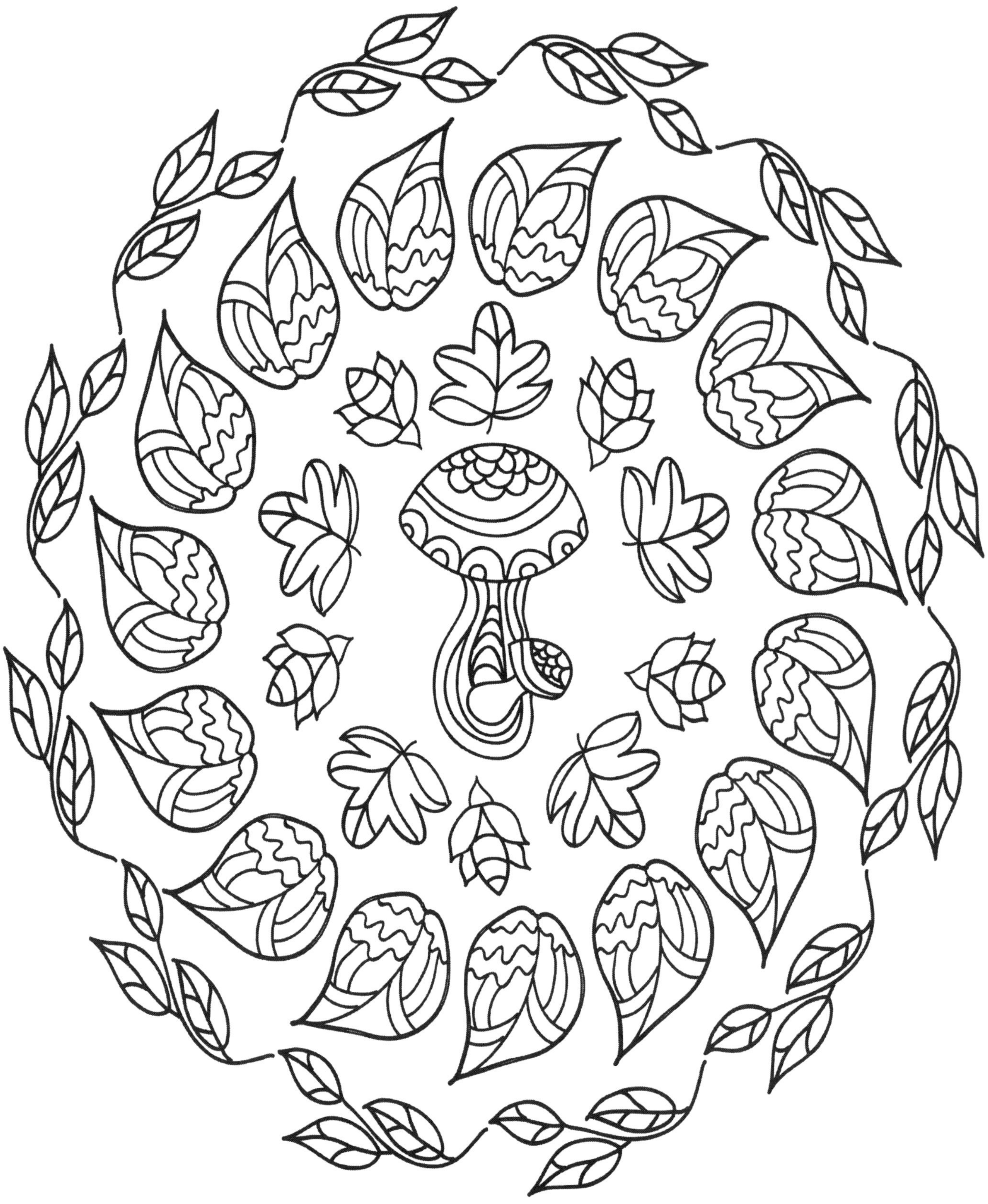

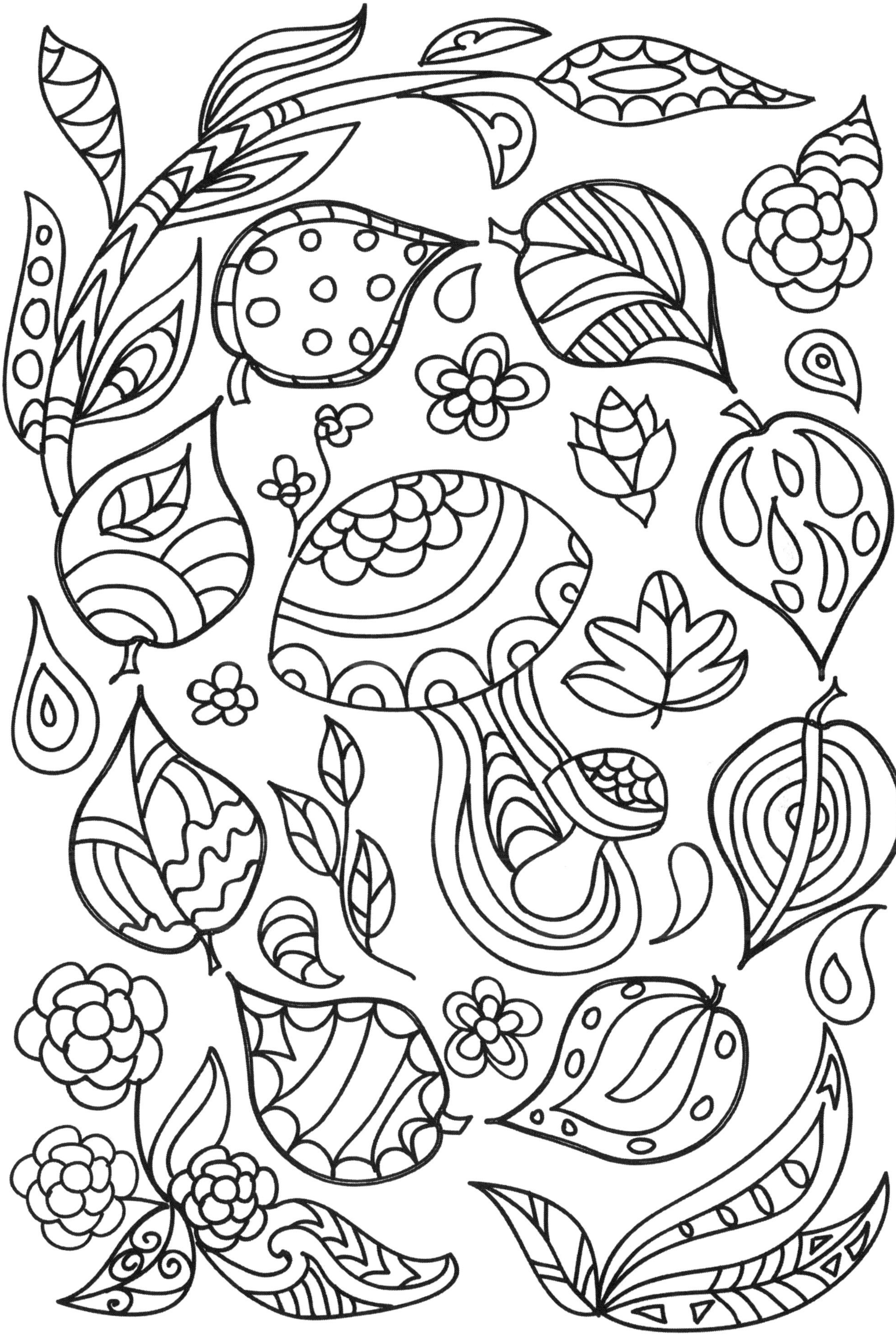

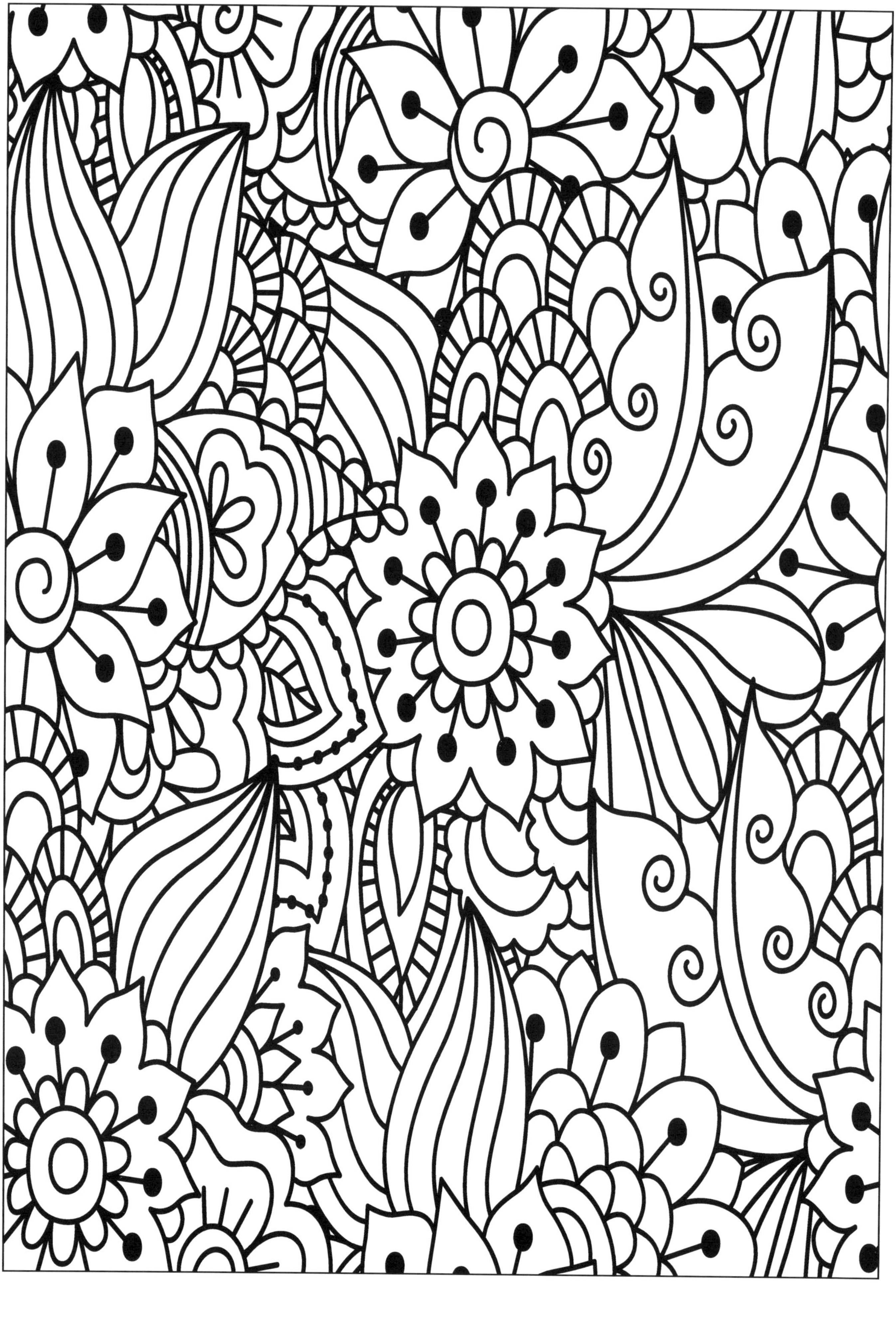

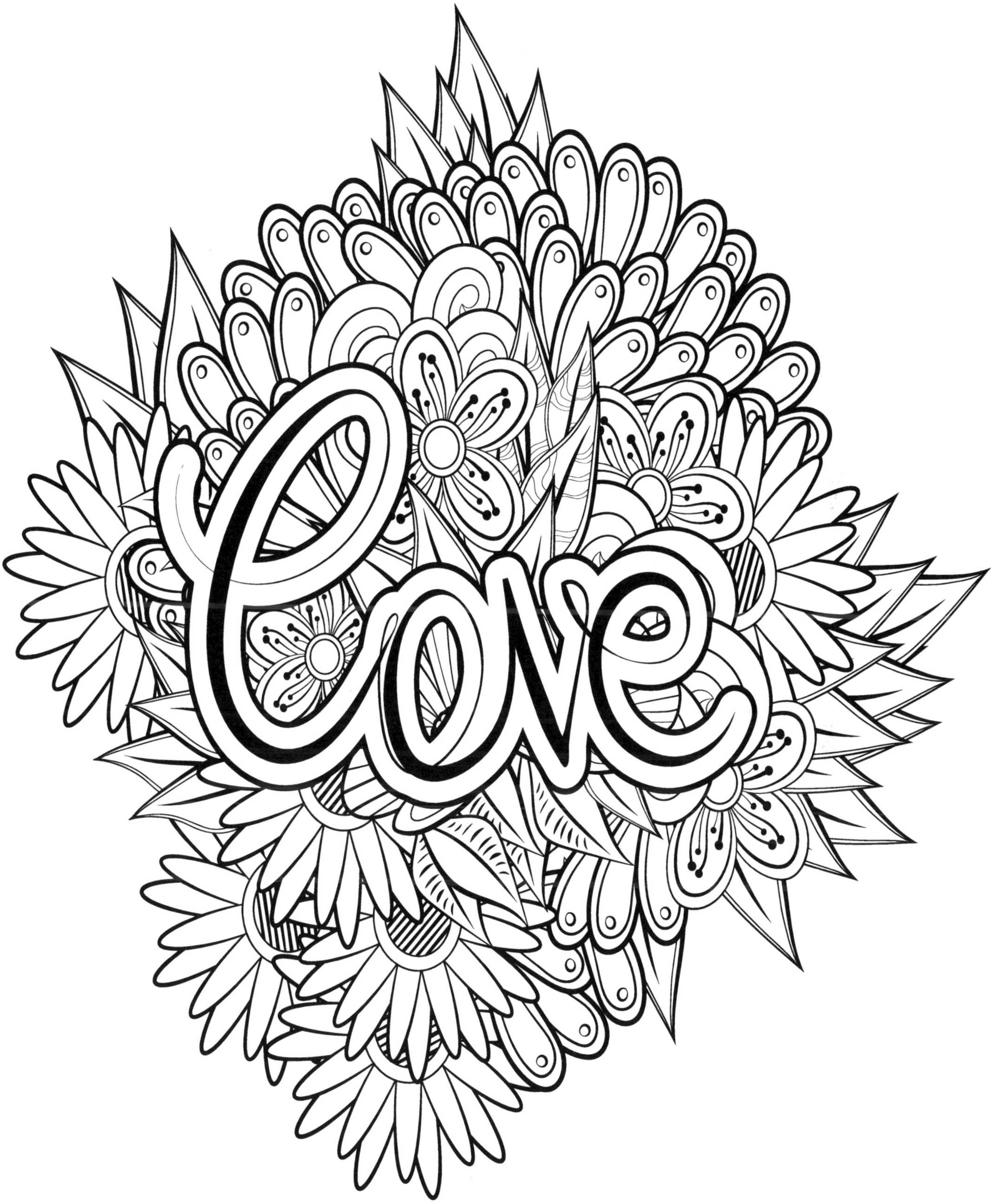
Love

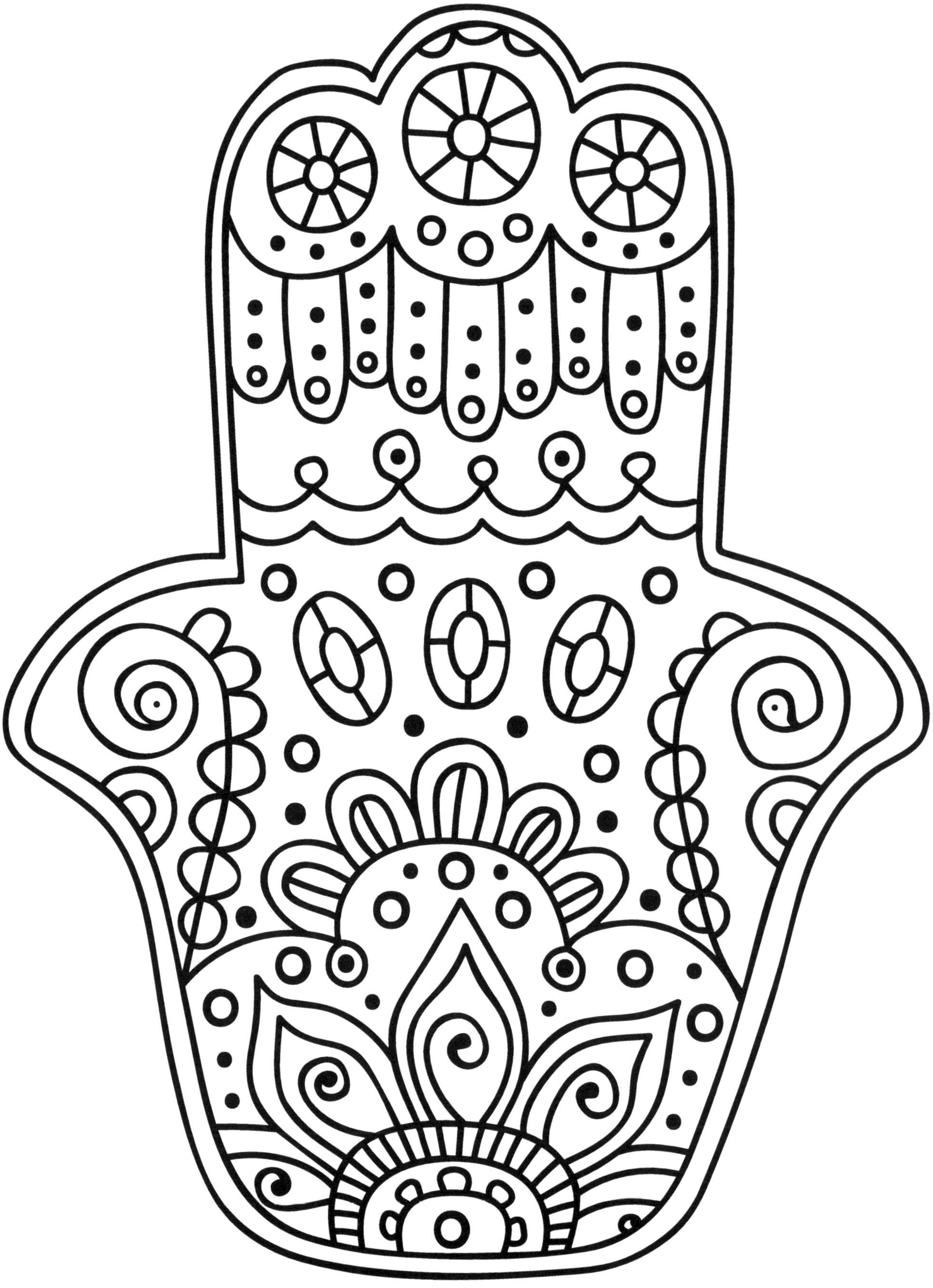

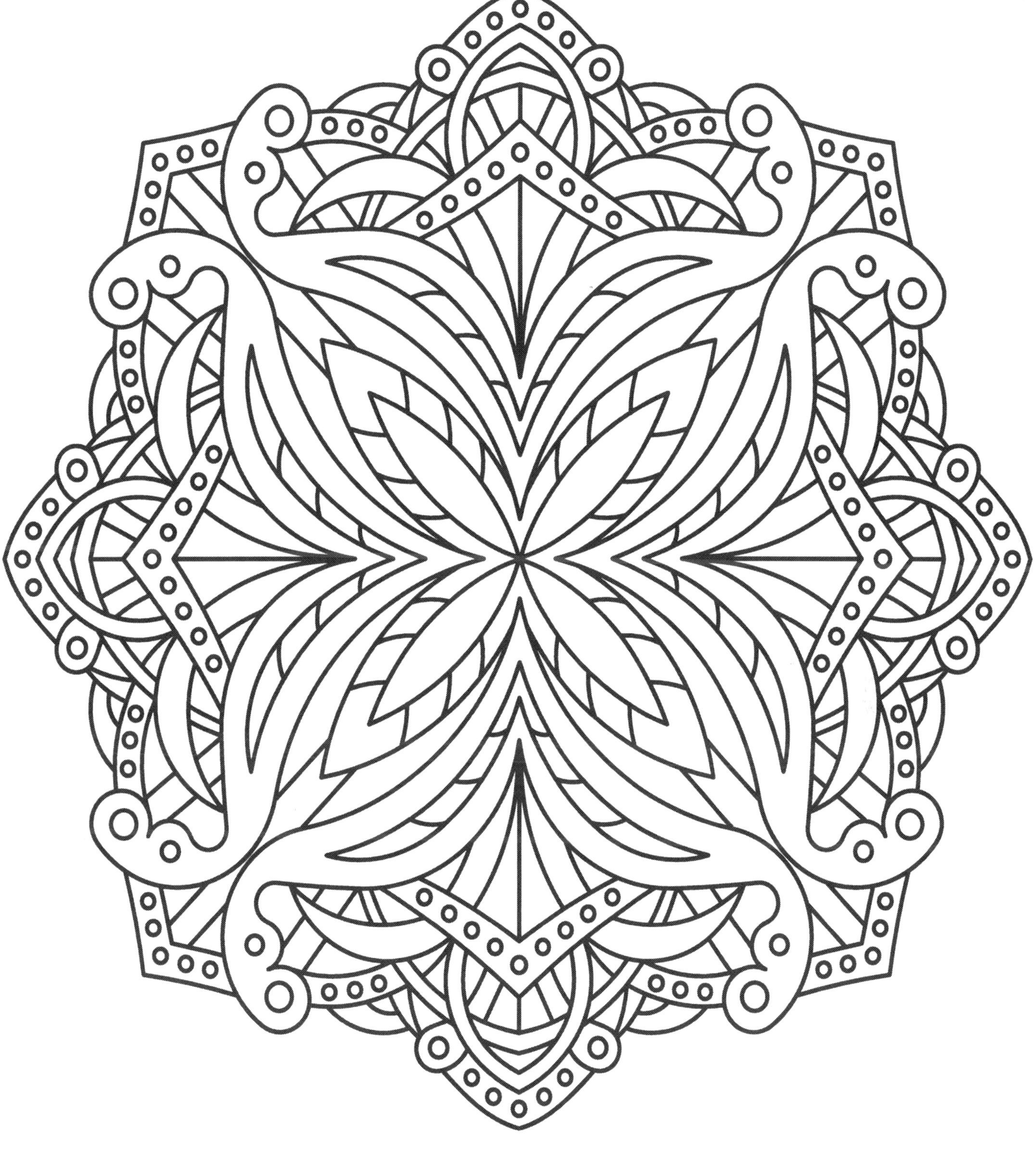

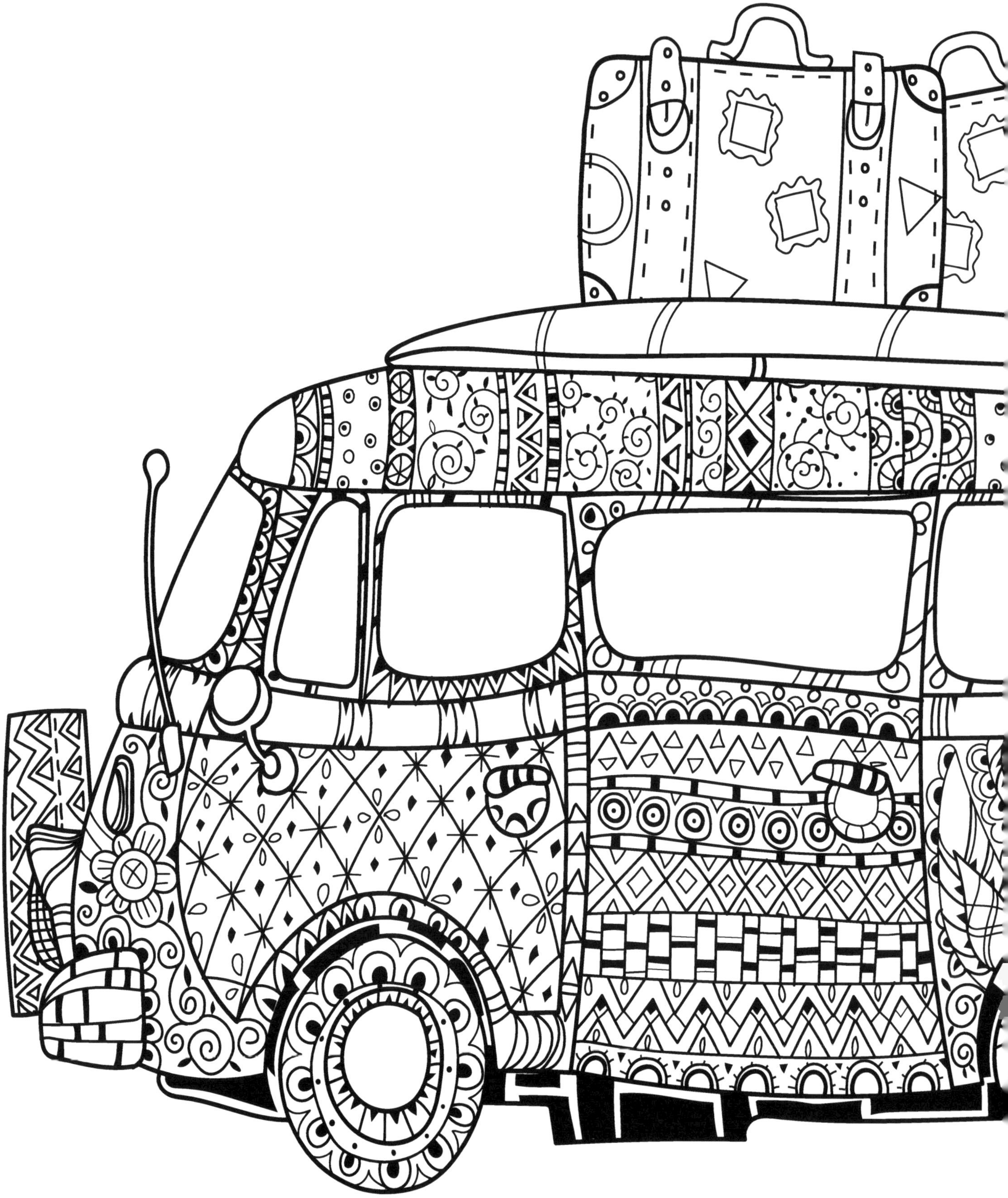

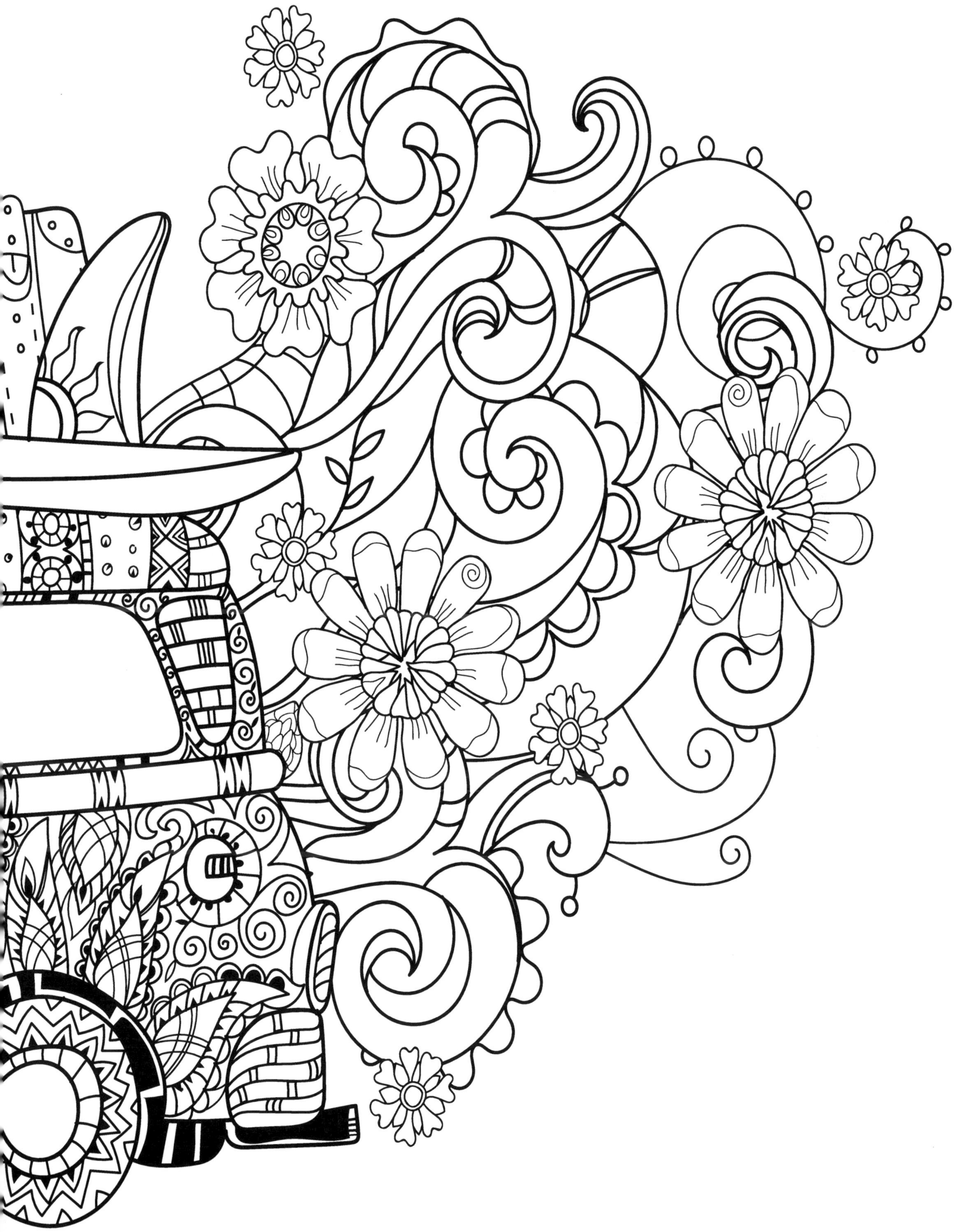

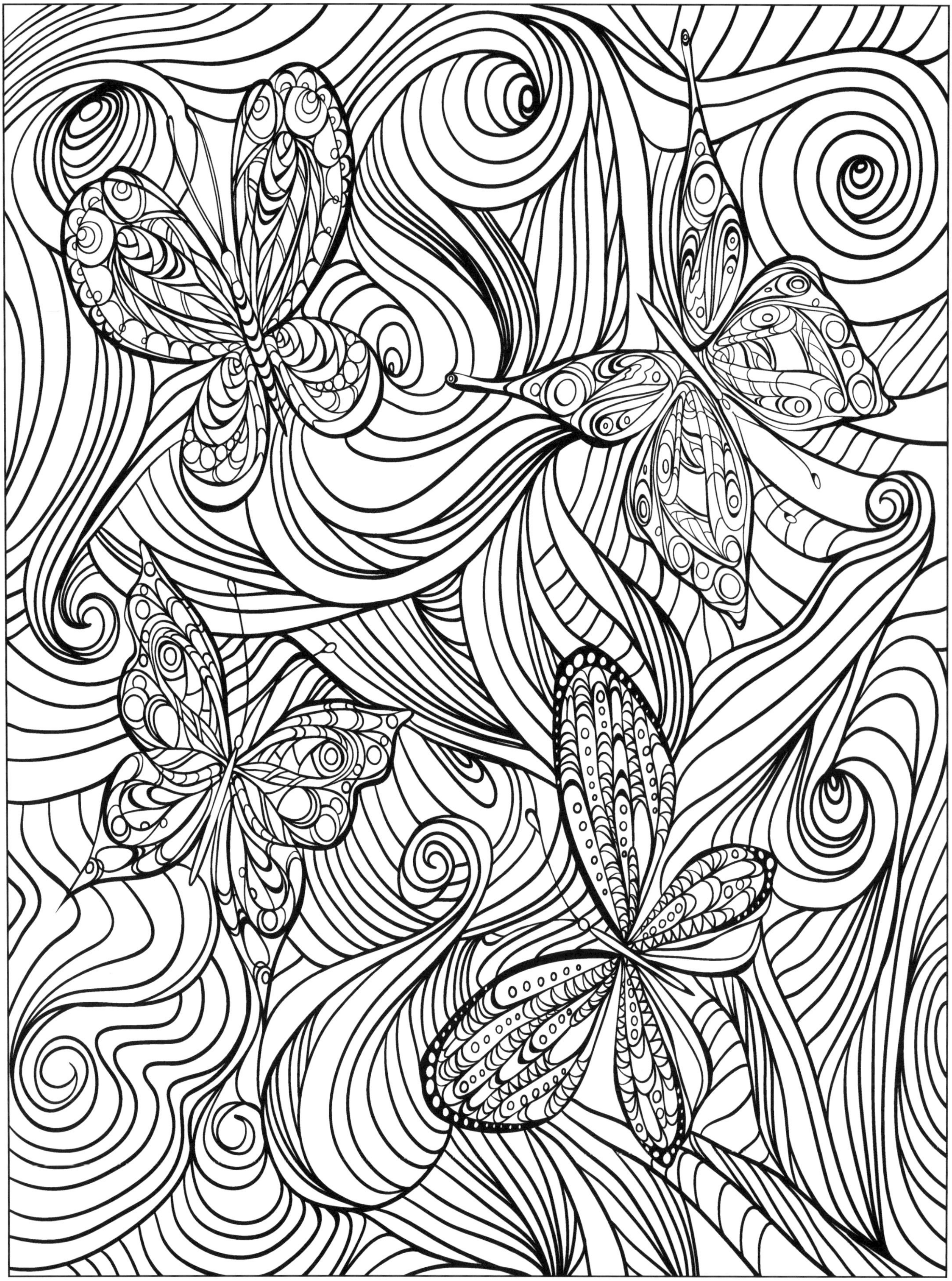

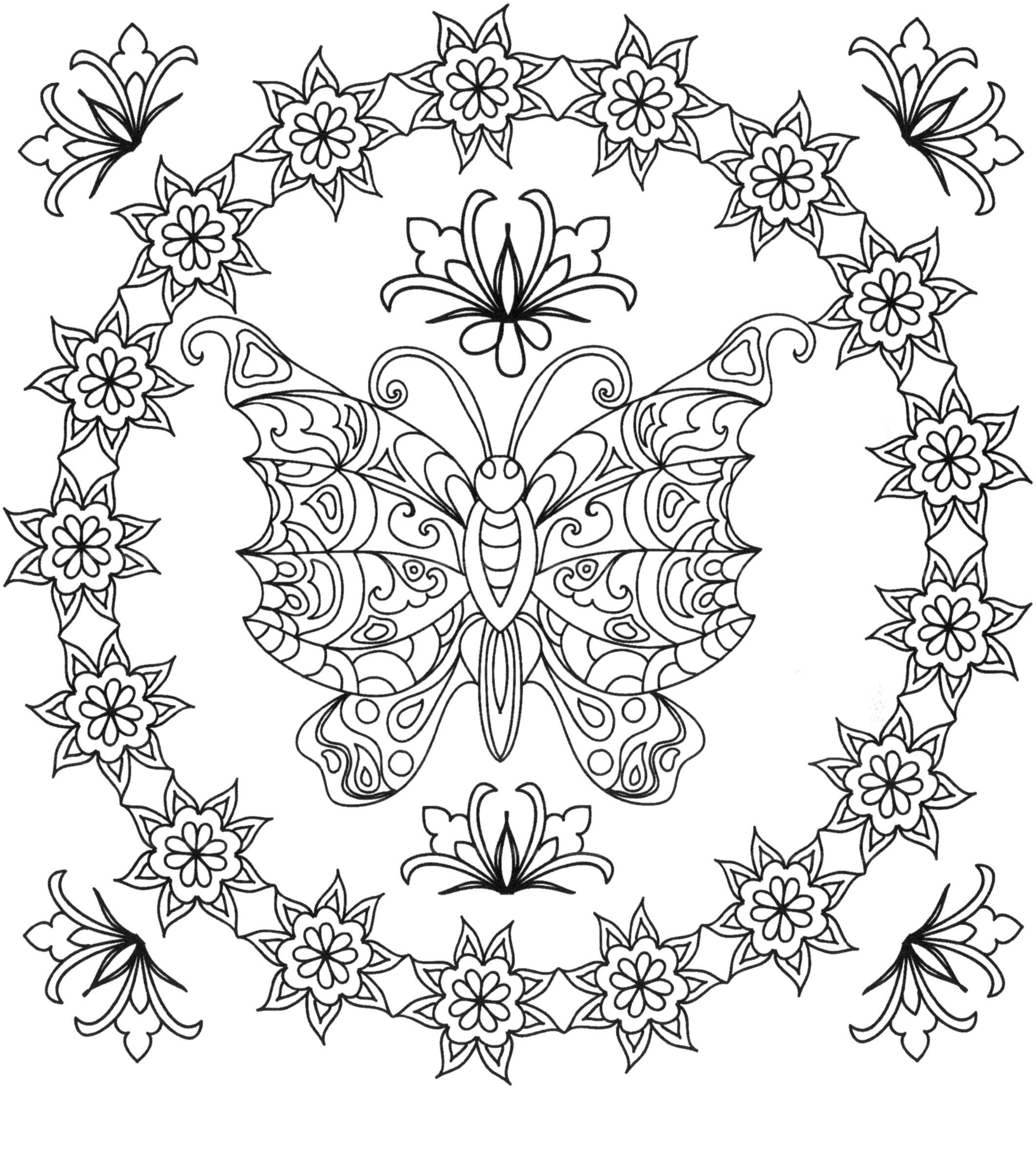

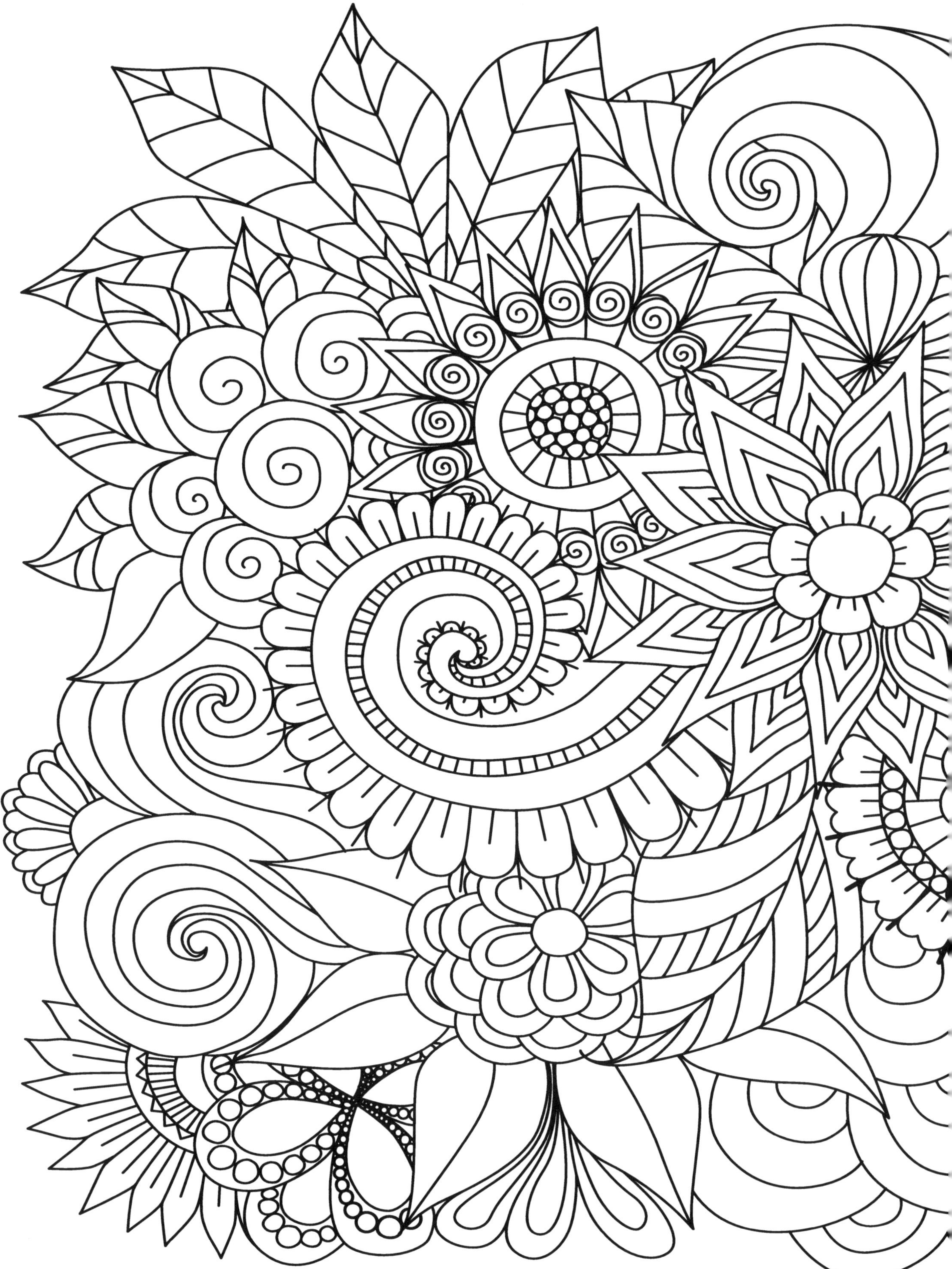

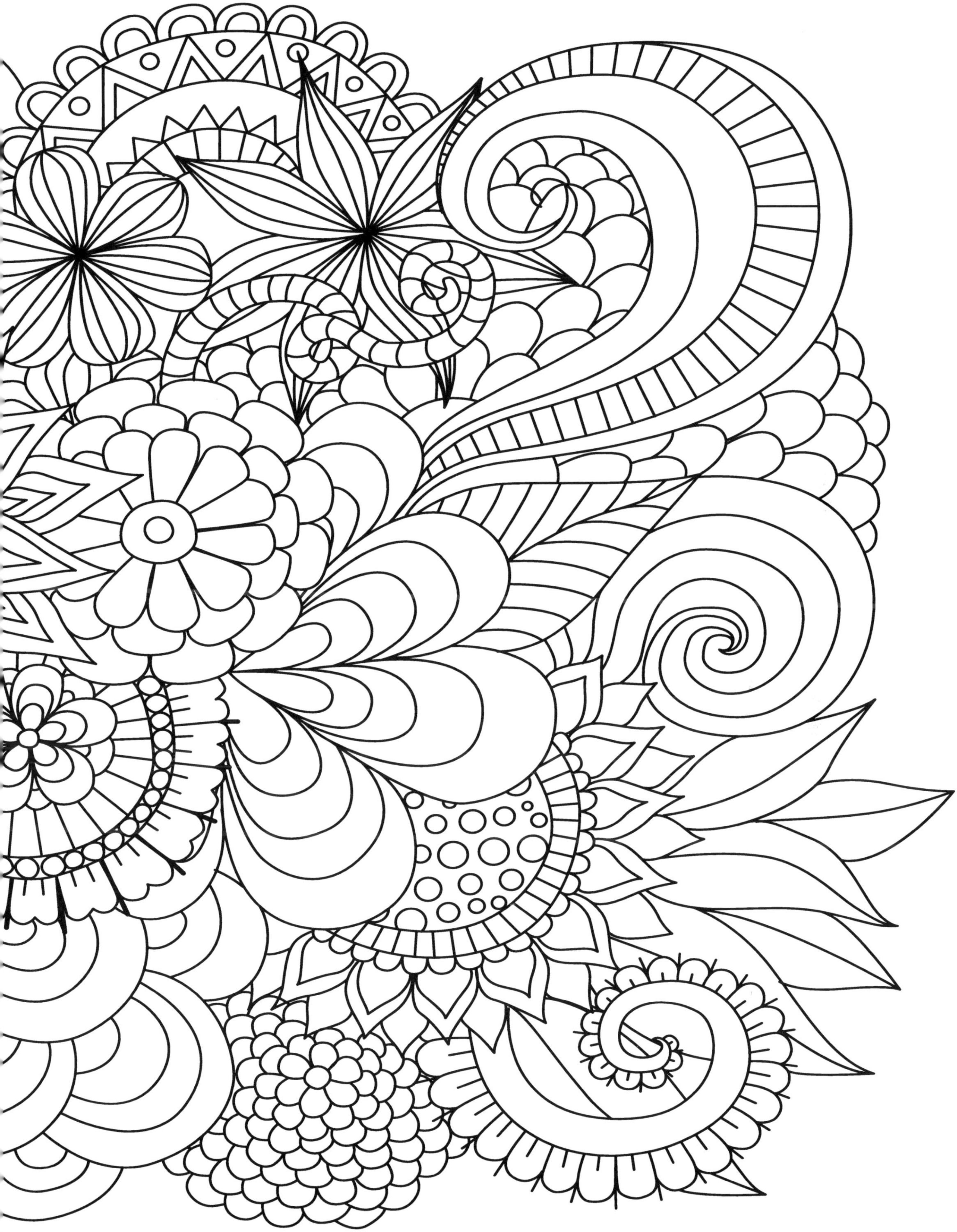

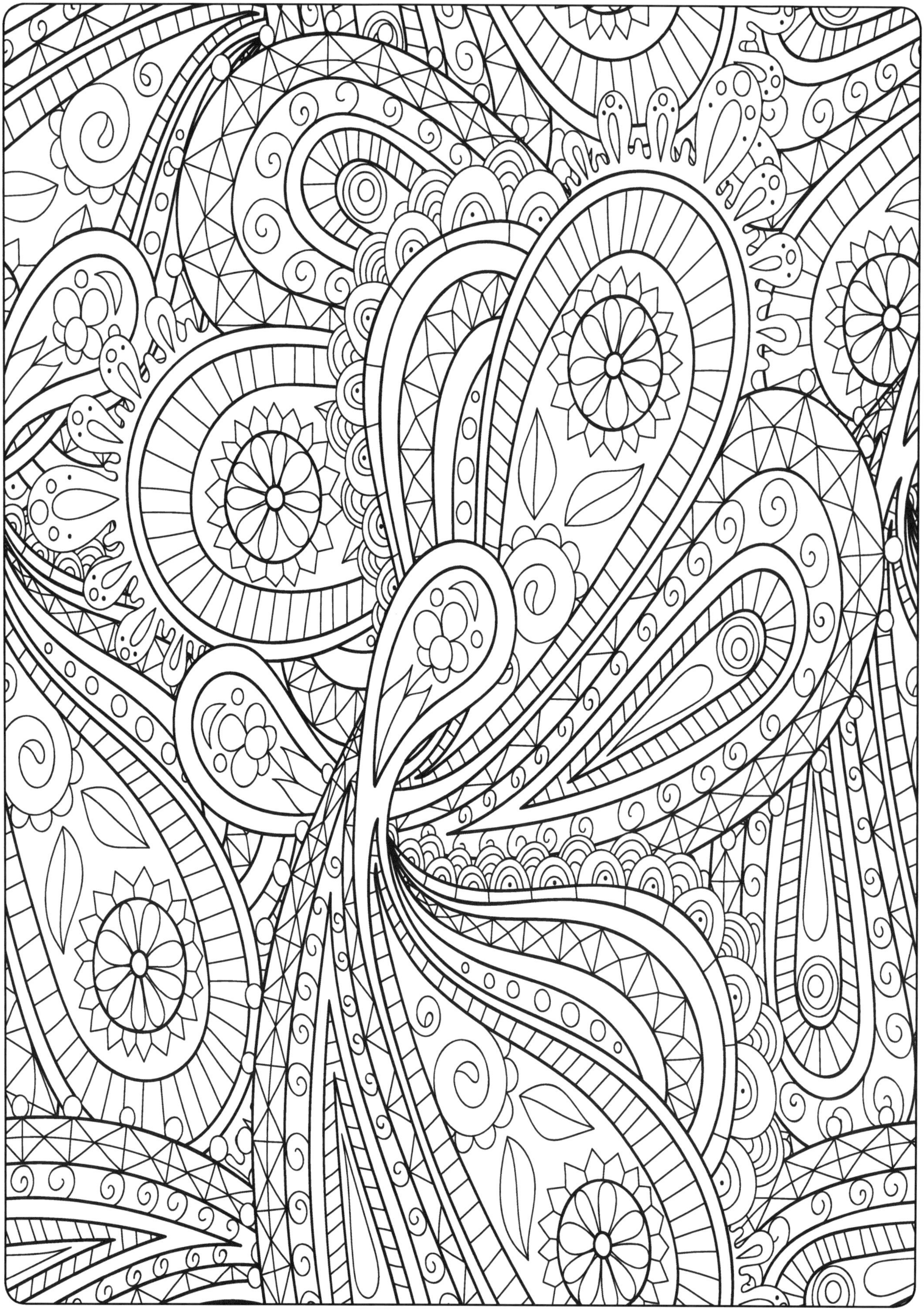

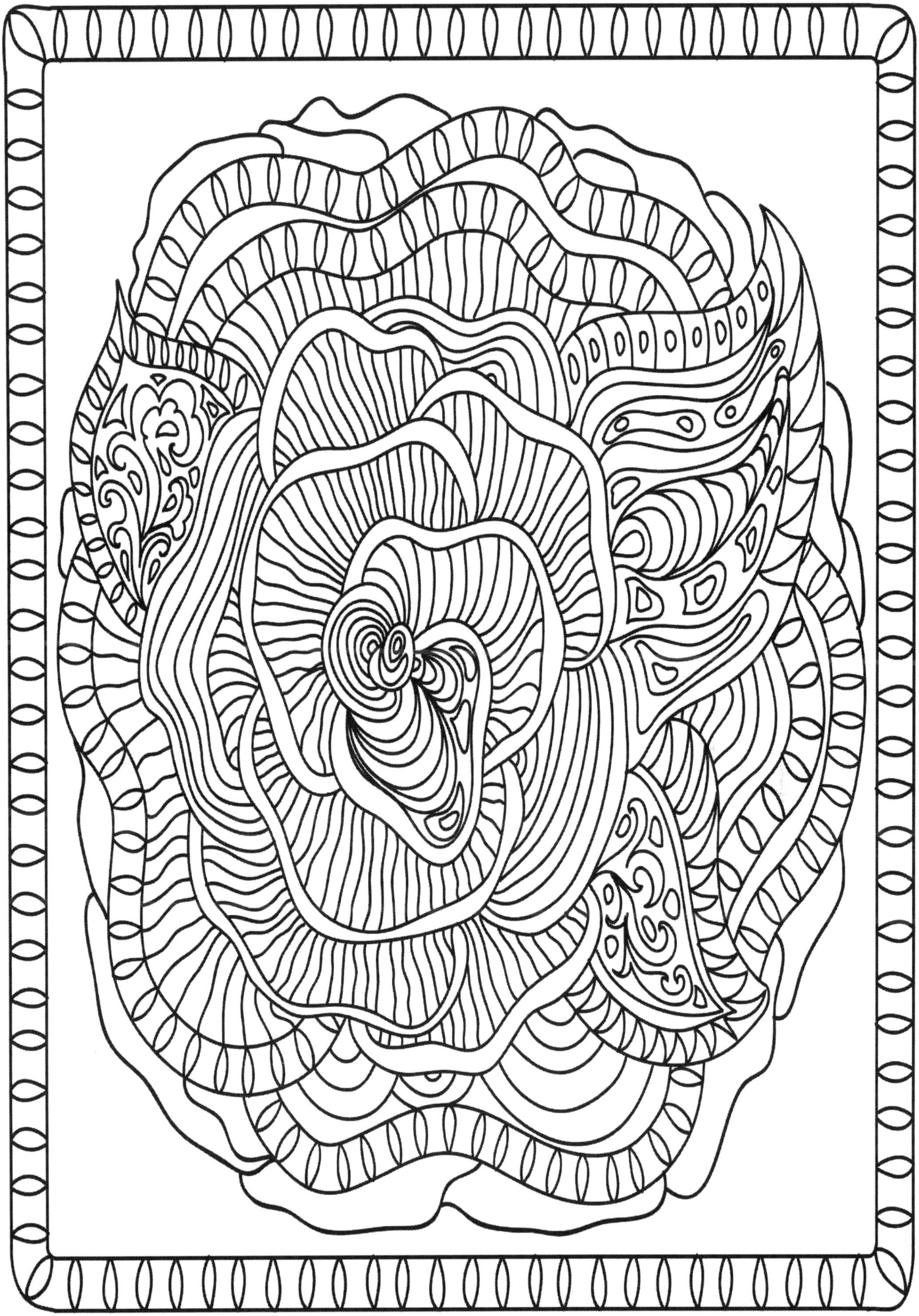

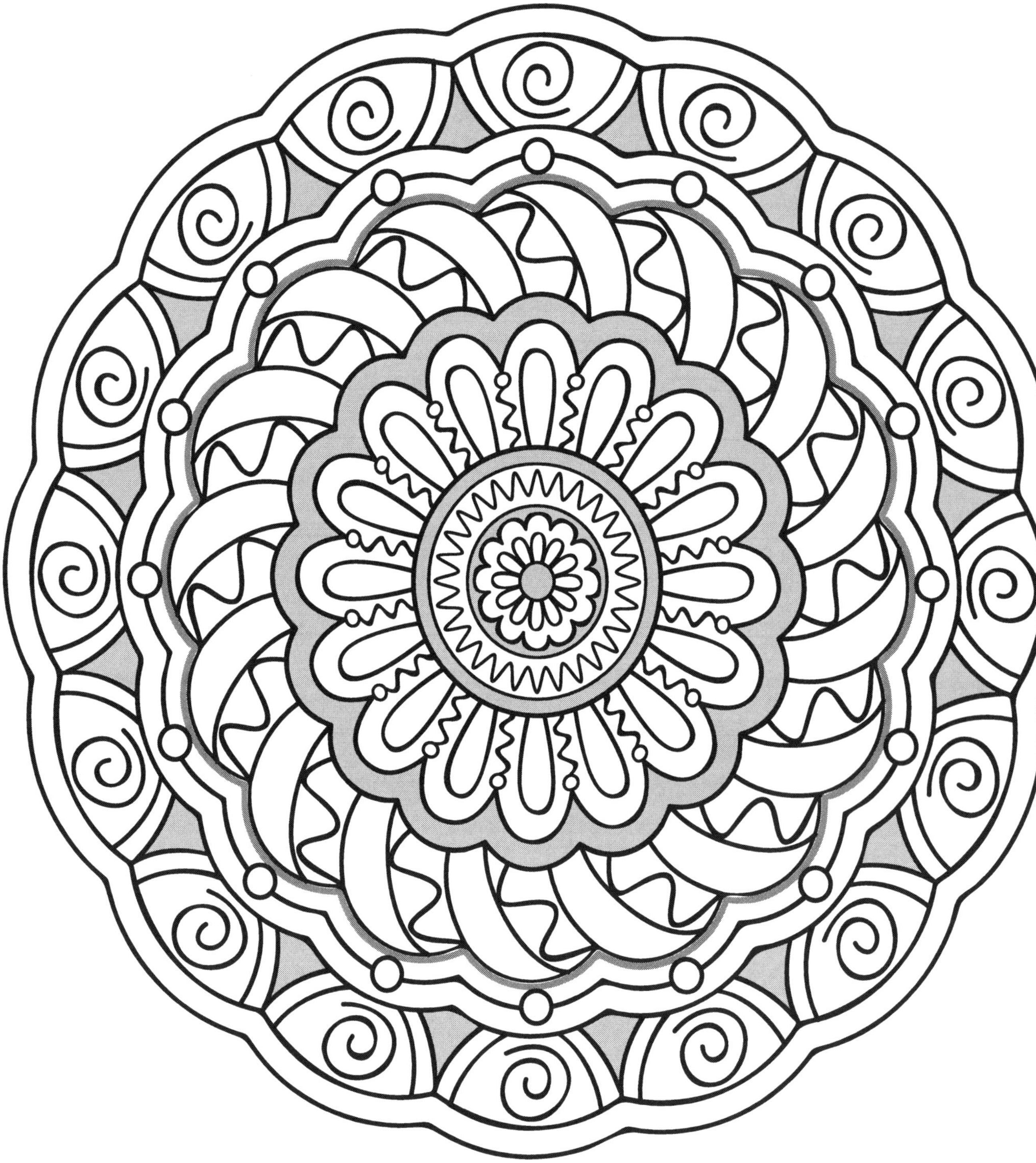

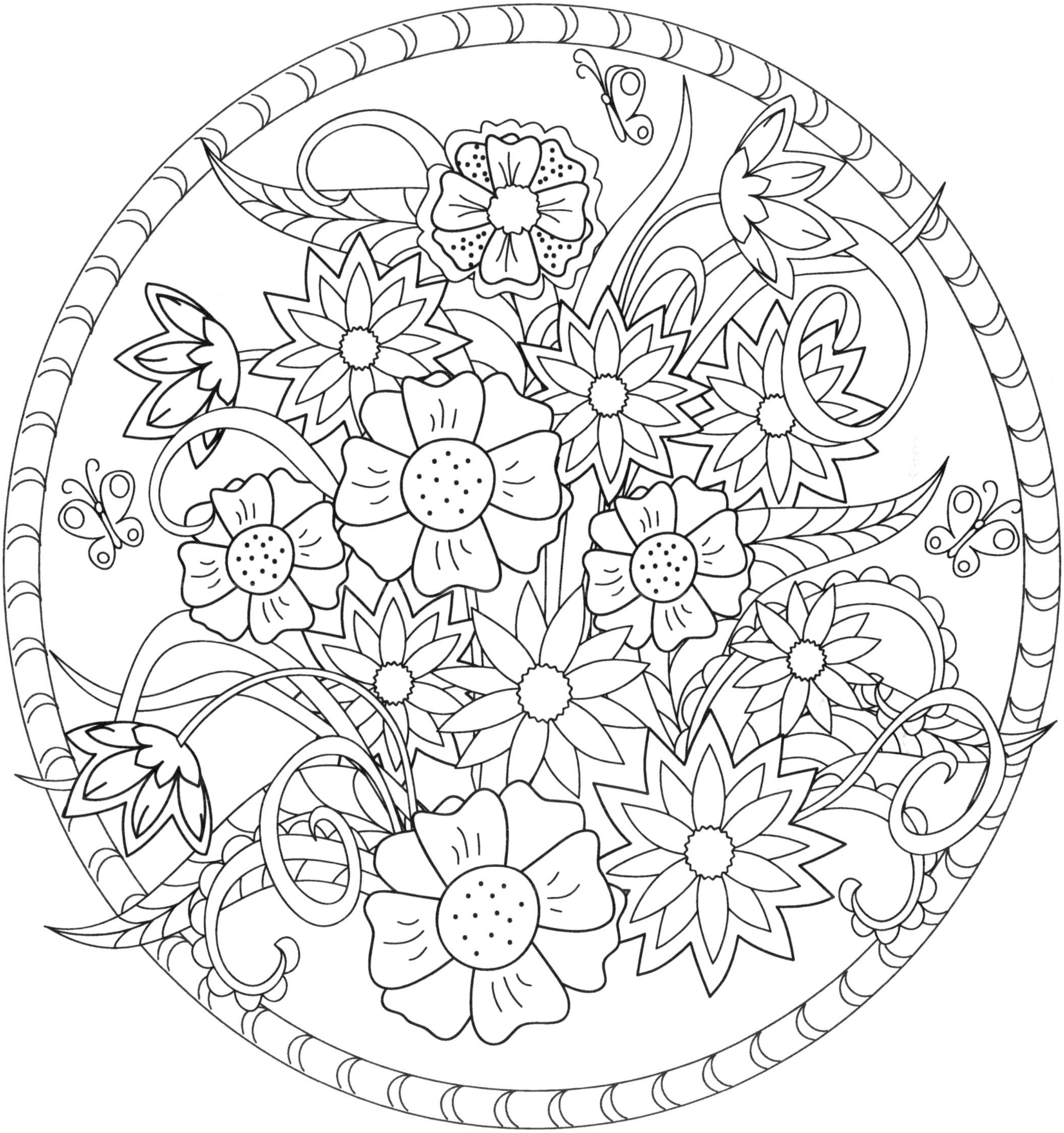

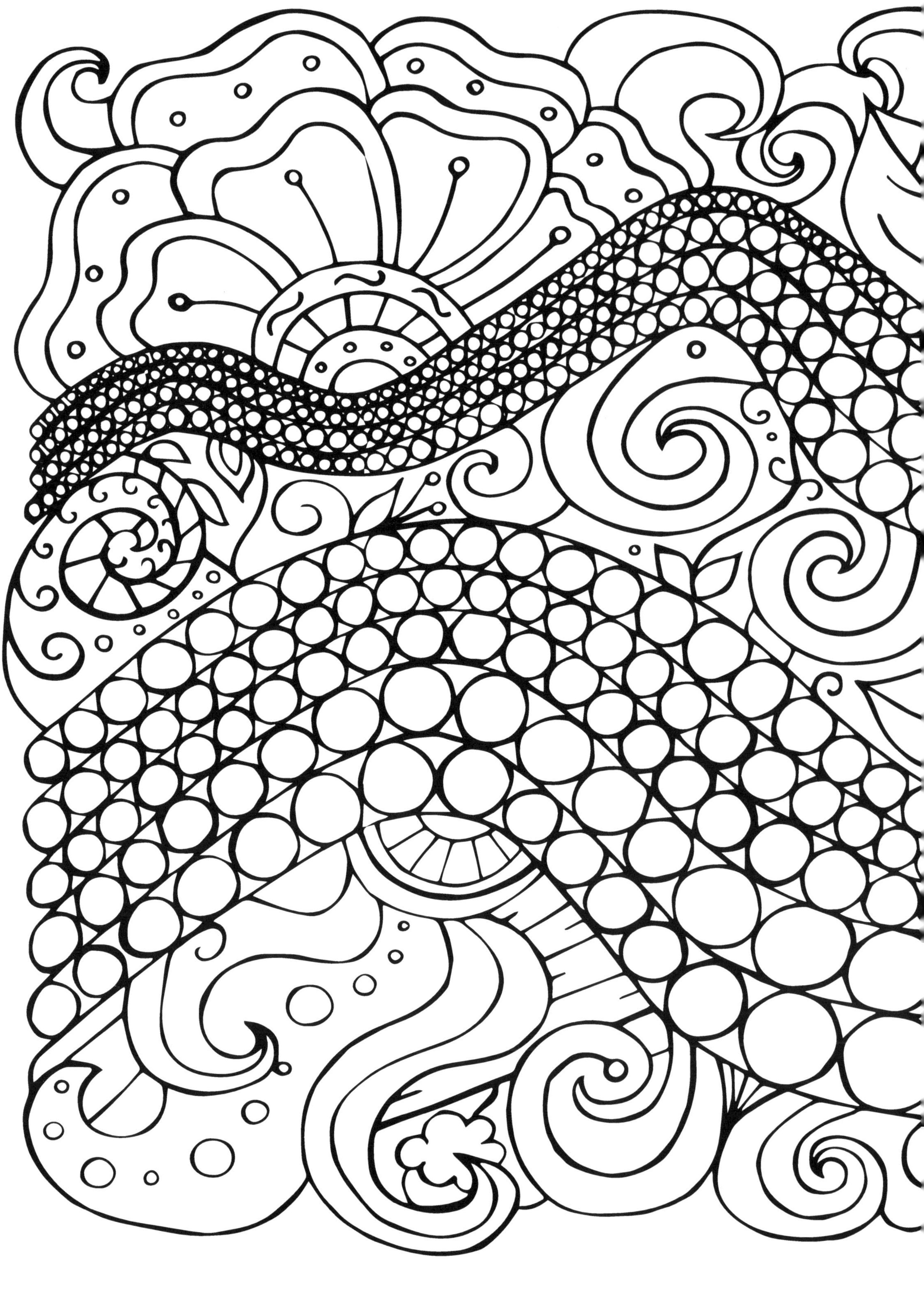

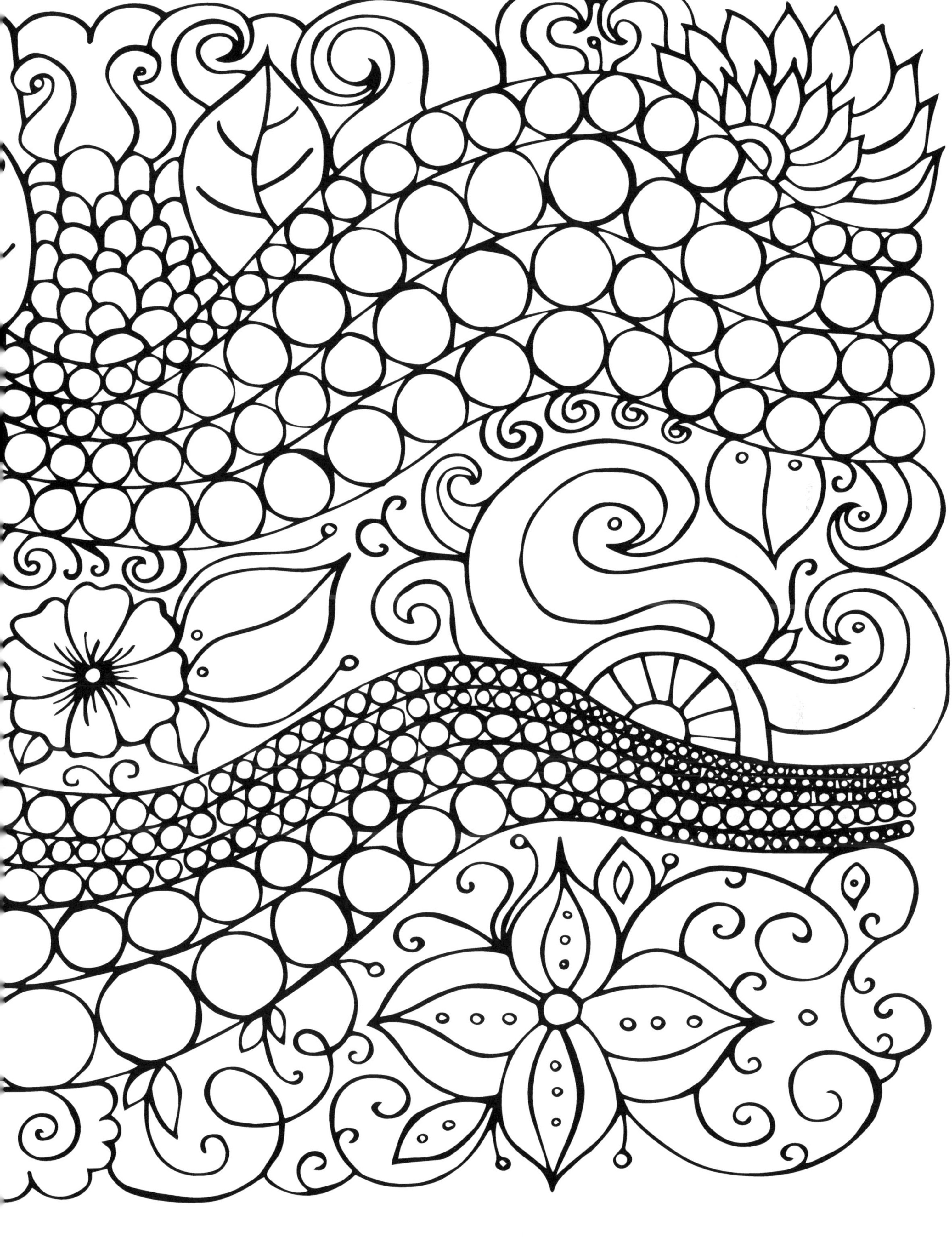

57703971R00020

Made in the USA
San Bernardino, CA
21 November 2017